Cyberpest

'**Cyberpet** /*n.* a hand-h[illegible]puterized toy which can be cared for at the touch of a button as if it were a real, live, demanding pet'

'This can't be happening,' said Rob. 'You know that. I know that. There just can't be a real live alien living inside this old cyberpet. It must be malfunctioning. Really. It's just a toy.'

Something strange happens when Rob gives Hatty his unwanted cyberpet. Somehow—even without a battery—the little toy seems to have a life of its own. At least, that's what his sister claims.

Before long Rob begins to wonder if Hatty is right.

Meg Harper is married with four children whom she educates at home. As well as writing, she enjoys reading, history, roller-blading and swimming. Her earlier novels *My Mum and Other Horror Stories* and *No More School* are also published by Lion.

For Phin, Jos, Kezia and Lydia,
with my love

Cyberpest

Meg Harper

LION
Children's Books

Published by
Lion Publishing plc
Sandy Lane West, Oxford, England
www.lion-publishing.co.uk
ISBN 0 7459 4195 8

First edition 1999
10 9 8 7 6 5 4 3 2 1

A catalogue record for this book is available
from the British Library

Typeset in 12/14 Bookman BT

Printed and bound in Great Britain by
Cox & Wyman, Reading

Contents

1

A Noise in the Night

Well, I finally said it. I finally told my parents exactly what I thought of them. And that was when all the trouble began.

'It's not fair! Rob always gets his own way but you never let me have anything I want! I can't go to the park on my own, I can't have a sleep-over, I can't watch PG videos—and I never get anything all the other kids have! No mountain bike, no roller-blades—not even a stupid little cyberpet! And Rob had three of those!'

That's what I said. As rudely as I could. Then I slammed out of the room and stormed up the stairs.

Nothing happened. You'd think it would, wouldn't you? You'd think someone would come and yell at me or something. But no. Nothing. That's what it's like, you see. They just ignore me.

'Oh dear, there she goes again,' they say. Or, 'Dear me, we never had all this trouble with Rob.' And Rob (he's my older brother, in case you haven't guessed) is just as bad. 'Don't get your knickers in a twist, Hatty,' he says. And yawns. My family is just so laid back, they're falling over.

So I thumped my pillow for a bit. Then I tried thumping the wall. I even got off the bed and jumped up and down for a while. Nothing. You see? They don't care.

But then something different happened.

The door opened!

'Shut up, Hatty,' said my loving brother. 'I'm trying to do my homework.'

'It's all right for you!' I growled. 'You get everything you want!'

'Oh yeah?' he said. 'So I had a mountain bike when I was your age? Dream on, Hat! You're just too young, that's all.'

'I'm not *that* much younger than you. I'm not too young for a cyberpet!'

'I paid for *those* myself!' said Rob, and he stomped out of the room.

But then something even more surprising happened. He came back!

'Here,' he said, and chucked something at me. 'Have this, if it'll keep you quiet. They're old news for year 6. We're into *Warhammer* now.'

I picked up the small plastic case and fiddled with the buttons.

'But it doesn't work!' I wailed.

'Get a new battery,' he said. And that was that.

Well, it's no fun staying in your room sulking all evening so, after a while, I stuffed the cyberpet under my pillow and forgot about it. Downstairs, no one seemed to have noticed I'd ever left. That's what it's always like. I could leave home and they'd probably just shrug and say, 'Never mind. She'll get over it.' Sometimes I feel like Matilda in that book by Roald Dahl. Too clever for this family. Trouble is, I haven't got any magic powers.

Or have I?

Maybe that's it? Maybe that's why it happened? Maybe it was me that did it? Maybe I should buy another one and see if it happens again?

Oh no! No way! I'm not going through that again! And anyway, don't kid yourself. It was nothing to do with you, Hatty!

Oh, so you know all the answers now, do you Rob? Why shouldn't it have been me? Huh?

It just wasn't and that's it, OK? And if you ever try to do it again, I'm not helping you. You'll be on your own. Got it? OK?

Oh, OK. Now leave me alone, can't you? How can I get on with this if you interrupt?

Aargh! You can't win in this house. When you're expecting a row, it never happens but when you just want a bit of peace and quiet, someone interferes. Wretched Rob has just been breathing down my neck, making snotty remarks about what I've put. I told him we had to write it all down or we'd never believe ourselves when we got old but he's only supposed to do his bits, not criticize mine. After all we've been through together you'd think he could be less irritating—but no. He's gone off in a huff now.

Anyway, this is what happened.

I went to bed, same as normal. Usually I say some prayers, but that night I was so tired I went straight to sleep. Not for long. Something woke me up. A strange little bleeping noise, a bit like an alarm clock, but not quite. I sat up. Was it the smoke alarm? No, it was in my room—in fact, it was coming from under my pillow!

So the battery isn't dead! I thought excitedly, rooting around for the little cyberpet. I couldn't find it and switched on my bedside lamp. The cyberpet slid off the bed and fell to the floor. The bleeping stopped.

'Oh no,' I groaned. 'It can't have broken.'

I peered at it anxiously where it lay. In the light from my lamp I could see very clearly. It was lying face down and there was no battery in its back.

'Bother!' I said. The battery must have fallen out. I crawled out of bed and started to rummage about on the floor. It could take me ages to find it. I was just reaching my hand under the bed when something stopped me.

The bleeping had started again!

'What?' I said and grabbed the cyberpet. Still no battery. And no bleeping either. I shook it. More frantic bleeping.

'I don't get this,' I said, peering into the back of the cyberpet. 'How can it be working?'

Then I turned it over. Which is when I got my second shock.

Instead of having a grey screen with a little black outline on it, the screen was pitch black—but down at the bottom a tiny multi-coloured blob was glowing at me. I shook it again. The blob bounced up and down.

There was only one thing to do. I went to wake up Rob.

'Uh?' said Rob and buried his head under the duvet. 'Go away, Hatty.'

'Rob, it's important,' I said. 'Your cyberpet's still working—but it's got no battery and it's all weird.'

'Oh shut up, Hatty. You've been dreaming. I chucked the battery away. I was going to get another but I couldn't be bothered.'

'But it's working, Rob! Come and look!' I was frantic with impatience.

'Go back to sleep, Hatty. I'll look at it in the morning.'

He burrowed even deeper into his duvet. There was no budging him.

Slowly, I walked back to my room. Could it

possibly have been a dream? Well, it was easy enough to find out. I only had to look.

But in my bedroom, all was quiet. No bleeping. I scooped up the cyberpet and was about to run back to Rob's room, when it let out a bleep fit to burst my eardrums.

'Aargh!' I shrieked and dropped it.

It lay very still and I froze. Had I woken the whole house?

Nothing. And then…

'Wha! Wha! Wha!' The bleeping went just bananas.

2

Enter Cyberpest

I snatched up the cyberpet, desperate to shut off the awful noise. I turned it over and over in my hands, pressing all its buttons, frantically trying to find a way to turn it off. Mum and Dad sleep like the dead but any moment now they would surely come storming in.

But it shut up anyway. Or at least the awful wailing bleep stopped and it seemed to whimper instead.

I stood in the middle of my room, clutching the thing to me, breathing hard. I peered at the screen.

No multi-coloured, glowing blob. Instead, sitting at the bottom of the screen facing me was a tiny, cross, multi-coloured alien. Well, I guessed it was an alien. What else could it be with its skinny rainbow body and its huge head that looked—well, angry? Its face was surrounded with great flashing spikes of colour. It was worse than looking at a strobe.

I shielded my eyes. Slowly the spikes faded a bit and began to droop. The bleeping stopped. And then started again.

My brain froze. The noise was beginning to build up. I couldn't stand it all over again.

'It's a cyberpet,' I told myself. 'What do you do with a cyberpet? You look at the icons, for goodness' sake!'

But there were no icons showing. I pressed the buttons randomly. The noise was getting louder.

'What d'you want?' I shouted at it. 'Are you hungry? Do you want some food?'

Immediately, the bleeping stopped.

Gently, I put the cyberpet down, then dashed out of the room.

'Rob! Rob!' I said urgently, shaking him. 'You've got to come and see this. There's a baby alien living inside your cyberpet and it keeps wailing at me.'

'Go away, Hatty. I'm asleep,' said Rob.

'But Rob, you've got to believe me. It's alive! Your old cyberpet's come alive!'

'You're dreaming, Hat. Go away.'

'Wait!' I said and scuttled back to my room.

The cyberpet was still lying on the carpet but when I picked it up, there was nothing there. The screen was still black but the alien had gone. I didn't dare shake it again.

I stood there staring at it and then ran back to Rob.

'Rob! The alien's gone but the screen's still black,' I said desperately. 'That's not right, is it? I don't know! I never *had* a cyberpet!'

He threw a book at me. 'Go *away*, Hatty!' he said. 'Tell me about your little green man in the morning! I mean it!'

I went back to bed, leaving the light on. The cyberpet lay black and silent in the middle of the floor. I was too tense to go back to sleep. What on earth was going on?

I lay still for what felt like hours, my eyes rooted to the spot where the cyberpet lay. In the end, I must have dozed off because when it did begin to wail, I couldn't work out what was going on for a moment.

Then I leaped out of bed and immediately started pressing buttons. I tried not to do it randomly this time, but it was difficult not to panic with the dreadful din building up again. What *had* worked last time?

'Oh, what did I do?' I muttered at it, stopping to try and think straight. 'I'm trying, honestly I am. I just need to find the combination that means food!'

The bleeping stopped. But I hadn't been pressing any buttons. Could it have heard what I said?

'Was it 'cos I said "food"?' I asked it. 'Was I imagining it, or did its skinny body look a bit fatter?' I tried again. 'Do I just have to say "food" to feed you?'

Yes, I was sure of it. It was definitely fatter than it had been.

'Food!' I said triumphantly. 'Food, food, food!' Fascinated, I watched it grow. And then there was a rather unpleasant noise; the little figure lurched to one side and a pile of something green and rather nasty appeared on the screen.

'Oh no!' I said. 'Don't tell me I've made you sick!'

But I had. The little creature set up a low moan and its lovely bright colours began to fade. All the little spikes around its face began to droop and its head began to look squashed.

'Doctor!' I said urgently. 'Nurse! Medicine! Tablets! Hospital!' I tried every medical word I could think of but none of them worked. The baby alien looked worse and worse. I cradled the cyberpet in my hand. It couldn't die! Not when it had only just come to life.

Sitting on the edge of my bed, I tried to think more calmly. When the cyberpet was hungry, it wanted food. Just like me. So what did I want when I was sick? My mum?

'Mummy?' I said experimentally. There was a little burst of moaning and a small glowing blob rolled down its face. Followed by another. And another. Oh no! Now I'd made it cry.

'I'll be your mummy,' I promised it rashly. 'And I'll make you better. Please don't cry.'

The moaning lessened a bit but it didn't stop.

Oh dear, what was I to do? The pile of nasty green stuff was looking even nastier. How on earth could I clean it up?

'Clean it up!' I said excitedly. 'I'll clean it up for you!'

At once, the pile of gloop disappeared.

Phew! I mopped my brow. But the little alien still looked poorly.

'Oh dear, it must smell terrible in there,' I said comfortingly. 'Would you like some fresh air?'

And that did it. The colours came back and the head went back to normal—except that the spikes had gone. I put the cyberpet down and breathed a huge sigh of relief. But immediately the wailing began again.

Oh no! I felt exhausted. What now? I peered at the screen. All the little spikes around its head were beginning to grow as the noise got louder.

Could it be hungry again? It had just thrown up everything I'd given it.

'Food?' I said nervously. The wailing lessened but didn't stop. I picked up the cyberpet and stroked it gently. I didn't dare try food again. 'Are you lonely?' I asked. 'D'you want a cuddle?'

The spiky head went smooth and for the first time the little creature's face puckered into what I thought must be a smile.

'There, there,' I said comfortingly, stroking it again. I climbed into bed and snuggled down with it still clasped in my hand. 'I'll look after you,' I told it. 'I promise.'

Little did I know what I had let myself in for.

3

Pest with a Capital P

At last! She's going to let me have a say! It's me, Rob, Hatty's big brother writing. Well, I didn't hear any more about the multi-coloured alien for a few days after that. In fact, I can't even remember Hatty waking me up on that first night, but she insists that she did and decided that since I didn't believe her, she wasn't going to tell me anything else. It was her secret.

She soon changed her mind. But then, who wouldn't? How was she to know that cute little alien was going to turn into Cyberpest?

Hatty began to behave very strangely. She was spending a lot of time in her room and looked tired out. She wasn't saying much either which was very unusual for her. We all noticed. Hatty thinks Mum and Dad never take any notice of her, but it's not true.

It is! Or it used to be.

No, it isn't, Hatty. They just don't make a song and dance about everything, like you do. Anyway...

If you're going to write rude things about me, I'll write it myself.

That wasn't rude; it's just true.

No it isn't.

Yes it is.

Isn't.

Is. You're doing it now. Making a song and dance. So there! Can I get back to the story now? Right?

'Are you all right, Hatty?' asked Mum, when Hatty had been drooping around for a whole day.

'Are you sure you're all right?' she said the next day.

That night Hatty woke me up, crying.

'Don't tell me to go away, Rob,' she begged. 'You've got to believe me this time.'

'Hatty, go and wake up Mum if you've had a bad dream,' I grunted.

'This is not a bad dream,' she insisted. 'Look!'

Grumpily, I reached out to switch on my bedside lamp...

And that's when I first saw Cyberpest. (Which is what we called it. At first.)

I took the cyberpet from Hatty and stared at the screen open-mouthed. Then I pinched myself.

'Wow!' I said. 'Where did you get this from?'

I didn't realize I was looking at a real alien, of course. I just thought Hatty had somehow got hold of some new generation of cyberpet.

'You don't understand,' wailed Hatty. 'It's your old cyberpet! I got it from you.'

I stared at it, dumbstruck.

The creature was bigger than when Hatty first saw it—but it was definitely still a baby. Its head was rather spiky and it stared out at me crossly. As I stared back, it opened its mouth and this unbearable wailing bleep began.

Hatty began to sob. 'I can't stand it, Rob,' she said. 'It keeps waking me up in the night needing food, or cleaning up, or cuddles—and at school it's a complete nightmare. Everyone's laughing at me. I mean, when they all had a cyberpet I didn't and now no one else has one except me! The first day I kept it on my lap so I could keep checking it before it began to wail, but the second day I got in terrible trouble. Mrs Sullivan said she knew exactly what I was up to and if I ever brought that cyberpet into school again, it would go straight in the bin.'

'So? Leave it at home, then,' I said reasonably.

'But I can't!' sobbed Hatty. 'It needs me. I promised I would look after it.'

'So? It wouldn't die if you left it on its own for just one day.'

'Yes, it would! Look at it! It's not going to be a baby much longer. It crawls around the screen

now and keeps trying to stand up. Three days ago it just slept and cried and needed cuddles. Its time is going much faster than ours! That's why it needs so much looking after.'

I could see what she meant. As I watched the wailing alien, it suddenly shuffled to the side of the screen and scrabbled at the wall, just as if it was trying to pull itself up.

'So if you leave it for a day, you reckon that's like leaving it for a few months?'

Hatty nodded dumbly and gulped.

Suddenly, I got a grip on myself. 'Hatty,' I said sternly, 'this can't be happening. You know that. I know that. There just can't be a real live alien living inside this old cyberpet. It must be malfunctioning. It can't die if you leave it for a day. Really. It's just a toy.'

'All right,' she said furiously and scrubbed at her eyes. 'You look after it, then.'

And with that she flung it on the bed and flounced out.

I didn't sleep a wink after that. As soon as Hatty walked out of the door, Cyberpest began to wail again. And, of course, I didn't know what to do. I pressed the buttons. I thought I knew all about cyberpets, didn't I? I'd had three. But that was a long time ago now. And pressing buttons didn't help. Could it possibly be a new design? The wailing bleep went on. At first I was too proud to go and ask Hatty what to do but before long the bleeping was unbearable. It wasn't that loud—not like a smoke detector, or even an alarm clock—but it got inside your head and drove you crazy. I ran to get Hatty.

Poor kid! She was fast asleep but I shook her awake.

Oh stop it, Rob. You make me sound like a baby!

Well, you looked like a baby, all curled up with your thumb in your mouth. But I didn't care. I was desperate.

Ha! You deserved to be.

I'll ignore that.

'Hatty! Hatty! How d'you stop the noise?' I yelled at her. 'Tell me quickly! I can't get the buttons to work!'

Hatty groaned. 'Just say what it wants,' she mumbled. 'If it's hungry, say "food".'

And then she turned over and very firmly pulled the duvet over her head.

Well, that sounded easy enough. I ran back to my room.

'Food,' I said firmly to the cyberpet. But the bleeping only got louder and more frantic.

What else could it want?

'Nappy change?' I said experimentally. It pulled a face and carried on wailing.

'Sleep?' I asked. 'A cuddle?' What else did babies like? I racked my brains. 'A walk in your buggy? Some toys?'

And then I hit on it. 'Your mummy? Do you want your mummy?'

For a brief moment, Cyberpest stopped its awful din and looked up at me trustingly. And then it started wailing all over again.

I ran along the landing. 'Hatty!' I said urgently, shaking her again. 'You'll have to come. I've tried everything I can think of but it wants you. It wants its mummy.'

Hatty didn't move. 'Tell it Mummy's busy,' she grunted. 'Now go away.'

'But Hatty…'

She sat up furiously. 'Go away,' she snapped. 'You must be dreaming. It's like you said. There can't possibly be a baby alien living inside your old cyberpet. And I want to sleep.'

I slunk back to my room. For a moment I thought the bleeping had stopped but Cyberpest must just have been drawing breath, or doing whatever it did to survive, because the moment I picked it up, it let out a furious wail.

'Mummy's busy at the moment,' I said, trying to be soothing. 'She'll be back soon. So I'm going to look after you for a bit, OK?'

The bleeping lessened a bit—it was more of an electronic whimper now—but I had this horrible feeling that any moment now it would be going full throttle again. And then I had an inspiration.

'Look, you're OK with me,' I told it. 'Honestly. I can look after you just as well as Hatty can because—well, you see, I know you haven't met me before but actually—well, I'm your daddy.'

4

It's Only a Toy!

Hatty wasn't speaking to me at breakfast. Well, she wasn't speaking to anyone, actually. She looked like a zombie.

And what do you think you looked like, nerd-brain?

Look, am I allowed to tell the truth, or do I have to be polite all the time?

Well, you don't have to call me a zombie.

I didn't. I only said you looked like a zombie.

Well, don't.

OK. No more zombies. And no more nerd-brains either, right?

Oh, OK. Get on with it then.

'Are you sure you're not sickening for something, Hatty?' said Mum, giving her a puzzled look.

'I'm just tired,' said Hatty. I was beginning to know the feeling. What was I going to look like

in a couple of days' time, if Hatty wouldn't have Cyberpest back?

Dad snorted from behind his newspaper. 'She's probably been staying up too late playing with that dratted old cyberpet that Rob's given her.'

Hatty jumped visibly. I tried to catch her eye. Like I said, you have to be careful with our mum and dad. They're not as dozy as Hatty thinks.

There was the usual rush to get ready for school but I managed to trap Hatty in the bathroom. I left Cyberpest to wail in my room.

'Hatty, you're not expecting me to look after that thing all day are you?' I demanded.

She looked at me witheringly over her toothbrush and kept me waiting until she'd rinsed and spat.

'What's the problem?' she said scornfully. 'It's only a toy!'

'But Hatty…'

She'd gone.

I caught her up just as she turned onto the main road. She's only little but can move very fast when she wants to. I felt like a lumbering ape chasing after her.

'Hatty, please!' I begged. 'I'm going to look like a real jerk. My class doesn't do cyberpets any more!'

'Neither does mine,' she said coldly. 'What d'you think it's like for me? My friends think I've gone mad!'

I decided to get tough with her. 'Look, you'll have to take this thing to school with you or I'll... I'll chuck it under the next lorry that comes along!'

'You wouldn't!'

'I would! Watch me!'

I pulled Cyberpest out of my pocket.

'No!' shrieked Hatty. 'Don't! Stop it. You can't kill it!'

'But it's only a toy, Hatty,' I said spitefully.

She snatched it out of my hand and clutched it against her chest. Tears were beginning to well up in her eyes.

'I'll take it,' she said quietly. 'Look, it's asleep. The screen's all dark. Maybe it'll stay asleep a nice long time.'

I felt uncomfortable. 'Hatty, I...'

'No, it's OK,' she said. 'I'll look after it. I promised I would. I said I would be its mummy.'

She slipped Cyberpest into her pocket and walked away quickly.

I followed her unhappily. What had I said to it, only a few hours ago? And I'd given up at the first hurdle! A fine dad I was going to be!

By lunch-time, I felt terrible. All morning I had thought of nothing but Hatty and how she was getting on with Cyberpest. Had she got in a row with Mrs Sullivan? Had Cyberpest ended up in the bin? What an easy escape that would be!

Except that Hatty would move heaven and earth to try to get it back. As far as she was concerned, it was alive.

When I'd eaten my school dinner, I strolled out into the playground, trying to look casual. I quickly spotted Hatty. She was sitting all alone in a corner near the rubbish bin. I felt dreadful. She doesn't have a special friend. She gets along with people all right but there's no one who stands by her when things get tough. Right now she looked very lonely and very miserable. I wandered over and stopped close by, pretending to sort through my pockets.

'Well?' I hissed.

'Dreadful!' she said in a low voice. 'It slept for ages but since then it's been wanting something every five minutes. I keep having to go to the loo. Mrs Sullivan said that if I'm no better after lunch, she's going to ring for Mum or Dad to fetch me home.'

'But they're both at work! We can't let her send for them if you're not really ill!'

'I know—but what else can I do?'

I made a difficult decision. 'OK,' I said. 'Hand it over.'

She didn't argue and the look of relief on her face was almost enough to make me feel good about it.

I was lucky. After driving me mad all lunch-time, Cyberpest settled down for an afternoon kip. The trouble started later. When it was time for football.

I'd just finished tying my bootlaces, when the bleeping began.

'Food?' I hissed at it. It shut up. Phew! That was easy. I couldn't put it in my shorts' pocket for fear it might fall out, so I shoved it down the back of my sock. I didn't think there was too much chance it would get kicked, as I usually play in goal.

All was quiet for the first ten minutes or so, and I was so absorbed in the game, that I forgot about Cyberpest. Then, just as the ball was heading my way, it let out a shrill bleep.

'Aargh!' I shrieked, jumping in the air in alarm. Someone booted the ball towards me and I hit the ground just when I should have been leaping to save it.

There was a chorus of groans from my team. 'Awh, Rob! That was an easy one! What were you doing?'

'What's the matter with you, Mattison?' said Mr Williams, our teacher. 'Got ants in your pants, or something?'

The only good thing about it was that everyone was going on at me so much that they couldn't hear Cyberpest, who was still shrieking.

'Sorry,' I mumbled and rested my hands on my knees, as if I needed a breather. I don't suppose they were convinced, as I'd hardly done

anything yet, but it gave me a chance to speak to Cyberpest. 'Food?' I tried again.

I was in luck. It fell silent.

It was a good five minutes later when Cyberpest bugged me once more. The play was in midfield. I dropped down quickly as if to check my laces.

'Food?' I muttered. 'Clean up? Drink? Toys?'

I didn't notice the striker bearing down on me until the yelling started. 'Wake up, Mattison! Watch the ball, you stupid berk!'

I leaped to my feet but was all wrong-footed and the ball zinged to the back of the net.

'Good grief, Mattison! What's wrong with you today?' demanded Mr Williams. 'Get your act together, for goodness' sake!'

'Yes, sir. Sorry, sir,' I grovelled, too relieved that Cyberpest had stopped shrieking to be much bothered.

But worse was to come. I made a couple of decent saves in the next ten minutes and thought rotten old Cyberpest had gone off to sleep. We were changing ends when the bleeping began.

'Ha!' said my friend, Mansoor. 'You'd better not let Old Willy catch you with that! He'll go bonkers. Anyway, why've you got it? No one's doing cyberpets any more. And I thought all yours were broken.'

'It's Hatty's,' I lied. 'She was stressed out 'cos

it was broken, so I brought it with me. Trouble is, it's not broken now.'

'Well, put it on pause,' Mansoor advised, as he ran to get in position. 'Or you'll have had it.'

Little did he know.

I pulled Cyberpest out of my sock and muttered my usual range of choices at it. And what did it want? A cuddle! Why words didn't work for cuddles neither Hatty nor I will ever know, but have you ever tried playing in goal, cuddling a cyberpet? All I could do was hope the ball didn't come my way. I was frantic.

'That's enough cuddles for now,' I kept telling it, but as soon as I tried to shove the wretched thing down my sock again, it began to wail.

And then the play moved up the field. I had a wild plan to try and head the ball away but as it sailed towards me, I automatically reached out my hands. Cyberpest soared into the air and landed with uncanny accuracy, right at Mr Williams' feet.

'Oh, I see,' he said sarcastically. 'So that's what the problem is, is it, Mattison? We'll talk about this later.'

And, with a deft sweep of his hand, he scooped up Cyberpest and put it in his pocket.

5

The Plan

'But sir, it's my sister's,' I protested. 'It was broken. I was only fixing it for her.'

The other boys were laughing and nudging each other. 'Ooh, diddums! How sweet!' I heard one of them say.

'Well, it's certainly fixed now, so it can stay safely in my pocket till the end of school,' said Mr Williams. 'Let's not waste any more time over it, please, Robert. And I expect to see you playing properly from now on.'

Well, how was I supposed to play properly when all the time I was worrying about Cyberpest? Supposing it fell out of Old Willy's pocket? Supposing someone trod on it? Worse, supposing it started to wail?

I tried to work it out. There couldn't be more than ten minutes until we had to go in and change and then it would be the end of school. Could Cyberpest possibly stay happy till then?

It didn't. As the players ran towards me, I could hear an unmistakable bleeping and Old Willy stopped to reach into his pocket. I saw him press a few buttons but, of course, the noise went on—and on, and on. He blew the whistle.

'Awh, sir, it can't be time yet,' several boys moaned.

'How d'you switch this dratted thing off, Mattison?' demanded Old Willy irritably.

Panic! I thought. What do I do now?

'Oh, it's easy,' said my mouth glibly.

It is? thought my brain.

I took Cyberpest in my hand and my mouth just carried right on. 'D'you want food?' I asked calmly, pressing buttons as if that would have some effect. 'Or is it some toys? Or perhaps it's a walk in your buggy?'

Phew! The bleeping stopped. 'There, sir,' I said, relieved enough to be cheeky. 'It's easy when you know how!'

'Humph!' snorted Old Willy. 'Just you watch your step, Mattison. It's time to get changed now, so you might as well have that thing back. But if I ever catch you with it in school again, it goes straight in the bin, even if it is your sister's. So be warned. Got it?'

'Yes, sir. Sorry, sir,' I said. I felt quite sick with relief. It's amazing what you can do in a crisis.

I waited for Rob at the end of our road. He'd have killed me if I'd hung around for him at the school gate.

'Well?' I shouted, as soon as he was close

enough. 'What happened?'

Rob said nothing. He just stomped towards me, with his hands in his pockets. It had been a disaster I could tell.

'Have you still got it?' I demanded.

He grunted. 'Wish I hadn't,' he said. 'Old Willy threatened to throw it in the bin if he sees it again and I'm sure Mansoor thinks there's something funny going on.'

We looked at each other in silence.

'Two whole days until the weekend,' I said miserably.

Rob nodded. I could see he was thinking about lorries again and what they might do to cyberpets. And then his face suddenly changed.

'Hey, Hatty,' he said, excitedly. 'I've just remembered. I was so fed up I'd forgotten. It's half-term after the weekend!'

'So?'

'So we've only got another two days of this.'

'I don't get it. What about after half-term?'

And then, before he said anything else, I realized.

Of course! After half-term, Cyberpest would be much older. In fact... I totted it up quickly in my head. I reckoned that three days of our time was about one year of Cyberpest's—so by the end of half-term, it would be... two, three...

'It'll be about five years old!' we said together, beaming.

Surely a five-year-old alien couldn't be as much trouble as a baby?

Rob kindly offered to look after Cyberpest that night. It's a good name, Cyberpest, isn't it? Rob claims it was his idea, of course, but really it was mine. He's gone off to play on the computer so he can't argue with that. Anyway, after that one afternoon trying to look after it, he was a bit shame-faced.

'Sorry, Hatty,' he said. 'Sorry I didn't believe you.'

'That's OK,' I said. 'Why should you believe me? You must have thought I'd gone bananas.'

'I did,' he admitted. 'In fact, I wish you had.'

'Thanks very much.'

'Oh, don't get huffy, Hatty! I only meant that then we wouldn't have to look after the wretched thing.'

'We? Are you going to help then? I thought...'

'Of course I'm going to help, stupid!' he snapped. 'I can't very well leave you to manage on your own, can I? Not now I know what a pain it is! I'm not a complete rat, you know!'

Hmmm, I thought. All this stuff we get at church about loving your neighbour must be paying off.

'So who's having it tomorrow then?' I asked innocently.

Silence. Then...

'You.'

Huh! So much for loving your neighbour!

'Thanks, Rob. You're a real help,' I said indignantly and was about to stomp off.

'No, wait, Hatty.' Rob looked screwed up with misery. 'Look, I can't let Old Willy see it again. Not after today…'

'So? What about Mrs Sullivan? And what about the other kids? I'll have no friends left at this rate. Everyone thinks I've gone mad!'

'No, listen. If you have it tomorrow, I'll look after it tonight and Thursday night and then on Friday, I'll have it, but I'll bunk off.'

'You'll what?'

'I'll bunk off. Skive. Play hookey. Not go to school.'

'But Rob,' I said, horrified. 'You can't. If Mum and Dad find out, they'll go crazy!'

'They won't find out. We can forge a note. Anyway, we've got a whole week to think up an excuse before any teacher is going to bother about it.'

I thought quickly. It was a good plan. 'OK,' I said. 'I'll skive too. Then we could pretend we were taking the last day off to go on holiday or something. Loads of people do that.'

'In October?' said Rob.

'Don't see why not. And don't look like that. I don't see why you should have all the fun. If you can skive off school, then so can I. But you can still have it for the next two nights.'

'But...'
'Either that or you get it tomorrow.'
Rob was cornered.
'Oh, OK,' he said, meekly enough. 'You win.'

6

A Dreadful Morning

Ha! And there you were thinking what a nice person Hatty was and that I was the bad guy in this story! Well, life is never that simple, is it? Our nice, straightforward plan to skive off school wasn't either. Of course, it was all Hatty's fault that it went wrong.

No it wasn't!

Yes, it was. If you'd gone to school like I thought you should, it would never have happened.

Yes, it would.

No, it wouldn't. When I realized I'd got no lunch I wouldn't have insisted on marching into Tesco's and buying some.

What would you have done then?

Starved.

I don't believe you. Who was it said, 'Brilliant! I'll get two Mars Bars!'?

Yes, but if you hadn't been there, I would

never have thought of it. So there. Anyway, who's writing this bit? You or me?

Oh dear, now Hatty's gone off in a huff. Well, she might not like what I've written about her but it's true, you'll see. Ha! No more Mr Nice Guy. I told you life is never simple, didn't I?

Thursday went smoothly enough. Mrs Sullivan had gone on a course so Hatty had a different teacher for the day. She has all the luck.

I didn't go off in a huff, actually. I just went to get a biscuit. And it isn't luck. It's 'cos I say my prayers.

Oh yeah. I'm sure.

It is. Try it if you don't believe me.

Huh! I suppose God sent Mrs Sullivan on a course just to suit you, did he? Come on, Hat! Get a grip! Can I get on with the story now, please?

It was easy at first. We'd worked out that it would be no good hanging around the park or something—someone was bound to see us and ask awkward questions. Nor was it any use trying to sneak back to the house, even though there is a key hidden in the garden. On our street there are a couple of old ladies who never miss a thing. So the problem was, where to go?

In the end, Hatty had an idea.

'The derelict houses!' she burst out. 'We could take some books and games and stay there all day. Then if it rains, it won't matter.'

'Are you crazy?' I demanded. 'Mum and Dad would have a fit if we went in there! And they're probably dangerous.'

'I don't see why. How can an old house be dangerous? And Mum and Dad'll go mad anyway, if they ever find out we've bunked off from school.'

So that was it. Secretly, I was dead excited. I knew there were older kids who hung around in the houses and some of my friends had explored them. I felt a bit of a wimp, never having even gone in.

The tricky bit was getting in without being noticed, but as the houses are on a triangle of land between the main road and a busy new one, it wasn't too difficult. The traffic moves fast and it isn't the sort of place where there are any nosy neighbours.

We didn't like it inside, though. It was smelly and dingy and there was loads of litter strewn about. It also felt a lot colder than outside.

'Ugh!' said Hatty, shivering. 'I don't fancy exploring. Let's just find a cleanish space and play a game.'

I didn't argue. Goodness knows what we

might have found if we'd looked too closely.

The morning seemed to crawl by. You'd think that a whole extra day off school would be wonderful—but it isn't if you've got to stay in a smelly, damp hole of a place with only a few books and games. It would have been great just to go outside and kick a ball about on the waste-land but we didn't dare.

By mid-morning, what with sorting out Cyberpest and putting up with Hatty whingeing on about what time it was, I thought I would go crazy. Good job she isn't here to see me write that.

'Oh, it must be lunch-time by now,' she said at last. We'd played all the games we'd brought and had started again. I was thinking of sneaking back home to get Monopoly. That takes for ever to play.

'No,' I said. 'It's only half-past eleven. We can't have lunch until...'

And then the penny dropped. Hatty and I looked at one other. We each knew what the other was thinking. We didn't have any lunch. We hadn't thought of bringing any because normally we have school dinners.

'We're going to starve!' wailed Hatty.

'Not in one day, stupid!' I said. 'We're just going to be hungry. It won't kill us.'

'But I can't just sit here thinking about food all day!' she protested. 'It's bad enough being

stuck here anyway, without being hungry as well.'

'You didn't have to come,' I said unfeelingly. 'In fact, it would have been a lot more fun if you hadn't. One kid is far less noticeable than two. I wouldn't have had to stay holed up here all day.'

'Oh yeah? And then what would you have done all morning, clever clogs?'

'I'd have thought of something. And at least I could have read my book in peace without you bleating at me every five minutes about what time it is.'

'You never said you wanted to read,' she snapped. 'Read your book now if you want to. I'm fed up with this stupid game anyway.'

And she tipped up our Labyrinth board so that all the little pieces slid off in a muddle. She can be very childish sometimes.

'Oh great!' I said furiously. 'Just you help me pick them up and count them. You know jolly well that if we lose a piece, it's ruined.'

'Pick them up yourself,' she said rudely and turned her back on me.

I felt like hitting her. I mean, we were only there because she wouldn't let me throw that blasted Cyberpest under a passing lorry and now she'd wrecked our game. I couldn't just leave it there until she helped me because it's my favourite game and I know what she's like when she's in a sulk. It can go on for hours.

That's not true.

Oh yes it is. Stop breathing down my neck if you don't like what I'm writing.

She only sulked for an hour, thank goodness. You have to admire her really. She's very determined.

There. Is that better, Hat?

Oh OK. Go on. Get on with it.

I picked up the pieces, then read my book and almost forgot about her. Cyberpest was quiet as well, so it would have been quite pleasant if it hadn't been so smelly and cold and my tummy hadn't been rumbling.

At last Hatty broke the silence.

'I'm starving,' she said.

'No, you're not,' I replied. 'Not like people in the Third World.'

'I'm not in the Third World,' she said, 'and I've just found my purse in my pocket so I'm going to go down to Tesco's to get something to eat.'

'How much have you got?' I demanded, quick as a flash.

'Just over two pounds. I'll lend you one, if you like.'

I didn't argue. It was too tempting.

'Brilliant!' I said. 'I'll get two Mars Bars!'

'Pig,' said Hatty. 'You ought to buy something healthy.'

'So what are you going to get?'

'An apple,' she said. And then grinned. 'And a Twix and a packet of crisps. D'you think I might have enough for a fizzy drink, as well?'

We didn't spend any more time arguing. The thought of food was too much. It was only when we were out on the road that I remembered we were not supposed to be seen.

'I've thought of that already,' said Hatty, when I worried at her. 'Loads of kids leave school at lunch-time to buy food or to go home for lunch. And we could always pretend it's a teacher training day, if we have to.'

She's not stupid, is she? In fact, sometimes I wonder if Hatty's a bit too clever for her own good. She probably really irritates the other kids.

Anyway, it wasn't far to Tesco's and it didn't take us long to choose what we wanted.

I started towards one of the 'ten items or less' checkouts.

'No,' said Hatty, grabbing my arm. 'Queue up behind that woman with the two little kids. We might be less noticeable.'

I thought it might be better to get out of the store as quickly as possible but it wasn't a bad idea. And it was Hatty's money we were spending.

The woman had a huge mound of shopping. My mouth was watering at the thought of my Mars Bars. I wondered about scoffing one and then paying for the wrapper, but I didn't have the nerve.

The mound of shopping seemed to be moving very slowly. One of the small kids began to cry. 'Want some sweeties! Want some sweeties!' he whimpered.

'I am sorry,' said the shop assistant, looking puzzled. 'The electronic eye just doesn't seem to be working. I'm having to type almost everything in.'

'I'd noticed,' said the woman irritably. 'Be quiet, James. You're not having sweets before lunch.'

James greeted that news by screaming and throwing himself on the floor. He was working himself up into a real tantrum.

'I'll call the supervisor,' said the assistant. 'It might be as well to change tills.'

'Oh great!' I groaned. That would take for ever, especially with James bawling for all he was worth. 'Come on, Hat. We'd better go to another checkout.'

'I don't think so,' said Hatty. 'Look.'

All the way along the store, lights were flashing above tills and shop assistants were looking worried. A woman in a suit was rushing from one checkout to another.

Suddenly, the loudspeakers buzzed and a voice said, 'This is a customer announcement. We are experiencing extreme interference with our computer system. We are hoping to resolve the problem shortly. We apologize for any inconvenience. Thank you.'

'Blimey!' I said, watching electronic gibberish sweep across the little customer display screen. 'It looks like the whole system's going down.'

'What are we going to do?' said Hatty. 'Wait?'

'We'll have to. I'm not going without my Mars Bars.'

Suddenly, Hatty grabbed my arm. 'Rob, look!' she said, in a horrified voice. 'Look what it says on the screen.'

Flashing past in quick succession were four multi-coloured words. They read:

Help! Where am I?

7

Caught!

Something about the colour of the letters was strangely familiar. Rob didn't catch on at first.

'What?' he said, looking stunned. 'Their computer's got serious problems.'

But I had a growing suspicion that it was nothing to do with their computer.

'No Rob!' I said urgently. 'Look what it says. And look at the colours. Cyberpest has hacked into their system somehow. I'm sure of it.'

'Don't be stupid, Hat,' said Rob. 'It can't have.'

Our eyes met. We were both thinking the same thing. Nothing seemed impossible now.

'Come on,' I said. 'We'd better get out of here before anything worse happens.'

And without even thinking about the food we were clutching, I pushed Rob towards the exit.

A heavy hand came down on my shoulder.

'Oh no you don't!' said a stern voice. 'We haven't all gone blind just because the system's down, you know!'

'Rob!' I shrieked, for Rob who had finally worked out what was going on, was already inside the revolving doors. He could have run for it, but he's not that bad. He came back. I suppose you could have worse brothers.

We both burbled at the security guard. 'We didn't mean it; it was a mistake—it was just that we forgot, what with all the tills going funny and...'

'Be quiet,' said the man. 'You can tell the manager all about it, when she's free.'

'But we can't wait,' I wailed. 'We've got to go back to school. It's our lunch-hour. Look, I've got the money here. It was just a mistake.'

It was ghastly. I could see the biggest row of our lives looming up. First skiving school and now being caught shoplifting. And all the time, out of the corner of my eye, I could see Cyberpest's multi-coloured message flashing past on the display screens. Rob looked like he might be going to cry and I felt much the same myself.

'Dear God,' I prayed frantically, under my breath. 'I know we shouldn't have bunked off school but we were only trying to look after Cyberpest. So please help us. Mum and Dad'll go mad if they find out about this. I'll never skive again, I promise.'

Another security guard came over.

'What you got there then, Bill?' he said. 'They're sharp these littl'uns, aren't they? Never miss a chance.'

'Yeah. The moment these two saw what was

happening, they were off like rockets. They claim it was a mistake, of course.'

'But it was!' I insisted. 'We just panicked.'

'Panicked? What's there for you to panic about? It's us that's got the problem, not you! You look over there now!' He pointed to all the frantic activity going on by the checkouts. 'Now that's what I call panic.'

'Well,' said the second security man. 'The boss won't want to see them right now. She's got enough on her plate. What are you going to do? Send them up to the office or let them off this time?'

'Please God, please,' I begged silently. I suddenly had an urgent need to go to the loo and my legs had turned to jelly.

The man who had grabbed me looked down at us consideringly. 'Well,' he said. 'I can't say you look like bad kids. I suppose it's just possible you're telling the truth... I'll tell you what. You can't pay for this stuff now anyway, even if you've got the money, so it'll just have to go back on the shelves...'

'But...' started Rob and then thought better of it.

'But if I ever catch you two up to any more funny business in here, then that'll be it. I'll tell the manager, your parents, the police... you get the message?'

We nodded dumbly.

'Right,' he said grimly. 'Give me the stuff and be off with you then. You'd better run or you'll be late for school.'

We didn't need telling twice. We ran.

We ran until we couldn't run any more. We didn't think about who might see us. We just wanted to get away and get Cyberpest as far from Tesco's as possible.

'Oh,' Rob gasped and collapsed against a wall. 'I think I'm going to be sick.'

'And I need the loo,' I panted and then forgot all about that because, to my complete horror, Rob began to cry.

'That was awful,' he sobbed. 'I thought he'd get the police. I thought...'

I put my arms round his waist. 'Don't cry, Rob,' I said firmly. 'People will notice us. And it's all over now. Come on. It's not far to the houses.'

Rob made a huge effort and scrubbed at his face.

'Sorry, Hat,' he said as we hurried along the road. 'Sorry about that.'

'Forget it,' I said, though secretly I was appalled. What was this Cyberpest doing to us?

'It was just that it was all my fault. Mum and Dad would have blamed me.'

'Don't think about it,' I said. 'It's all right now.'

Suddenly, I was filled with an uncontrollable fury. I snatched Cyberpest out of my pocket.

The screen was blank.

'Don't pretend you can't hear me!' I raged at it. 'And if you're asleep, wake up. I don't know what you think you were playing at back there, but I've had enough. HELP! WHERE AM I? indeed. What were you trying to do? We look after you, don't we? We've even skived off school because of you. And you nearly got us in the worst row of our lives back there. If you can write messages, why haven't you done it before? Well, too late, Cyberpest. You've had it now!'

And I raised my arm to throw it into the oncoming traffic.

'No!' shouted Rob and grabbed my arm. 'You can't do that. Not now!'

But he was too slow. I had already opened my hand and Cyberpest was sailing out into the middle of the road.

8

A Narrow Escape

As soon as I'd done it, I regretted it and stood petrified with horror, watching the traffic zoom past. Cyberpest had landed between the white lines which marked the two lanes on our side of the dual carriageway.

'Idiot!' screamed Rob. 'What did you do that for? It can send messages now! It might be able to answer our questions!'

'I was just so mad,' I said, my eyes rooted to the spot where it lay, missing being crushed by a hair's breadth every time a car passed.

'We'll have to get it back,' said Rob. 'If we leave it there it'll be murder.'

I didn't argue. This wasn't the time to ask how you could murder a piece of plastic. And anyway, he was right. And I would be the murderer.

'But how?' I demanded. 'I don't see how we can.'

'Traffic lights,' he said.

Of course! There were traffic lights near the derelict houses where the new road joined the main one. Any moment now, they would change and the traffic back here would begin to slow, even if it didn't stop. It should be easy for one of us to dart out and rescue Cyberpest.

But we didn't have time to wait. 'Crikey, Hatty!' gasped Rob. 'That one's changing lanes!'

And before I had time to work out what was going on, Rob dashed straight into the path of a car which, sure enough, was crossing lanes and was right in line to crush Cyberpest to smithereens.

I screamed, then shut my eyes and prayed, waiting for the inevitable thud. I was convinced Rob had left it too late. There was a great blaring of car horn and a skid of tyres and I opened my eyes again to see Rob waving at me triumphantly from the central reservation. The driver couldn't stop immediately, but his indicator was flashing. He was going to pull over.

'Quick, Rob,' I yelled, 'the driver's coming back.'

For the second time, Rob ran across the road, but this time the traffic was slowing for the lights and it was pretty safe. Mum and Dad would have thrown a fit if they'd known, of course. We've had road safety drummed into us since we first learned how to walk.

The furious driver was now running towards us. I grabbed Rob's arm and dragged him off down a side-street. If I didn't go to the loo soon, I was sure I was going to burst, but there wasn't time to think about that now.

We ran as fast as we could, all thought of not being seen forgotten. We were heading for the park.

'We can't go to the park,' panted Rob. 'Someone might see us!'

I was too breathless to reply and just ran on. As if it mattered where we went now! We just had to get away. Surely the man wouldn't follow us very far?

But he was very determined and very, very angry. When I glanced behind, he was gaining on us. I started praying again. It was getting to be a habit.

The park gates loomed ahead of us and I suddenly had a brilliant idea.

'The loos!' I gasped. 'He'll never follow us in there!'

'Why not?'

'Because we'll go into the ladies, idiot! Come on!'

'I can't...'

'Oh yes you can!' I panted. 'Stop arguing.'

And we tore across the grass, past the play area and into the dank, cold, ladies' loos.

'Go in one and lock the door,' I urged Rob. 'In case someone else comes in.'

He did as he was told.

I've never been so glad to see a public loo in my life. I leaned against the wall of my cubicle and listened to my heart hammering. Next door

I could hear Rob gasping for breath. After a few minutes, I felt better. We must have shaken off the angry driver. Unless he was waiting for us outside.

'Rob,' I hissed. 'I'm going to see if he's gone. Stay there.'

I washed my hands innocently and then stuck my head out of the door. No sign of the man. Perhaps he'd given up at the park gates. But coming towards me was a woman with a small child.

''Scuse me, love,' she said and I quickly stood out of her way. There was nothing I could do. Rob would just have to stay in the loo a bit longer.

But it wasn't that easy. Suddenly I heard the woman's voice.

'Are you all right in there?' she was saying. 'You don't sound very well.'

I bounced back into the loos.

'It's my sister,' I explained brightly. 'She gets asthma. She's probably just using her inhaler. You're OK, aren't you, Roberta?'

Rob grunted.

'She'll be fine in a minute,' I added cheerfully.

'Are you sure?' said the woman. 'She sounds terrible to me. I'm a nurse, you see. I wouldn't like to leave someone having an asthma attack on their own.'

'Oh, we've just been running around a lot,' I said, panting. 'I'm very breathless too.' That, at least, was the truth and I could see that the woman was beginning to believe me.

'Well, I'll just wait a moment until she comes out,' said the woman. 'Better safe than sorry, you know.'

I could see no way of escape. Any moment now the woman would realize that we ought to be in school.

'Have you finished, Roberta?' I said urgently. 'This lady wants to check you're OK.'

'I'm fine,' said Rob, who was breathing normally now. I could tell that he was trying to make his voice a bit higher.

There was a moment's wait and then he opened the door. I mean, there wasn't much else he could do. I thanked our lucky stars that we don't have school uniform and that jeans and a sweater do just as well for a girl as a boy.

But the woman wasn't fooled.

'Hmm,' she said, suspiciously. 'You do seem a lot better now but I must say Roberta seems a very funny name for a boy.'

9

Lost!

At that precise moment, I could have killed Hatty.

Soon changed your mind though, didn't you?

Yes, all right, clever-clogs, I'm coming to that. Now push off and leave me alone.

Good. She's cleared off. Anyway, let's get this absolutely straight. I do not look like a girl. Some boys do, but not me. For a start, I have my hair cut very short and although I was due for a hair-cut, it still wasn't exactly girlish. I could think of nothing whatsoever to say.

Hatty could, though. 'Oh,' she said, crossly. 'Take no notice, Roberta.' She turned to the woman. 'You've hurt her feelings now,' she said. 'She used to have really long hair, but she had to have it cut very short and she's very sensitive about it. And my mum says people shouldn't make personal remarks.'

The woman looked embarrassed but not convinced. 'Oh,' she said. 'What happened? Was she in an accident?'

'No,' said Hatty stoutly. 'She just had a terrible attack of head lice. A real infiltration.'

'Infestation,' I muttered.

'That too,' said Hatty, glaring at the woman and scratching her own head suggestively.

'Oh, I see,' said the woman, drawing her small daughter towards her. 'So didn't the treatment work?'

'No,' said Hatty firmly. 'They were super-lice.'

Then she grabbed me by the arm and dragged me out of the door.

'Don't run,' she hissed. 'Look casual.'

'You ought to go on the stage,' I growled.

'Yes,' agreed Hatty. 'I was brilliant, wasn't I?'

And she began to skip. Why I didn't kick her, I don't know.

It still wasn't the end of school-time. I think that Friday was the longest day of my life. There was nothing for it but to go back to the derelict houses and hide for a bit longer. I was worn out, fed up and very hungry. All we needed was to meet some busybody friend of Mum's. Right that minute, I wished I'd left Cyberpest to die in the middle of the road.

Hatty was full of beans, though. She was extremely pleased with herself.

'Well,' she said, as soon as we were back in our dank hole with our pile of games. 'That was pretty clever of me, wasn't it?'

'Stop gloating,' I snarled. 'Anyone can tell lies. It's nothing to be proud of.'

Hatty had the grace to look crestfallen and we sat in silence for a moment or two.

It was then that something very odd struck me. Why was Cyberpest so quiet?

'Hey, Hatty!' I exclaimed, quickly feeling my pockets. 'Did I give Cyberpest to you?'

'No,' she said. 'I haven't seen it since I threw it into the road. You haven't…'

But I had. 'I've lost it!' I wailed. I stood up and frantically turned out my pockets. Suddenly the thought of some other kid picking it up was unbearable. No matter what a pain it was, this was our adventure. We simply had to get it back.

'You stupid berk,' said Hatty furiously. 'How can you have lost it?'

'Shut up!' I snapped. 'I didn't say anything when you threw it in the road!'

'Oh yes you did! You called me an…'

'Well, never mind that now. We'll have to go and look for it. Come on.'

This time we walked. I don't think we could have run if we'd tried but, anyway, we had to search. We prodded at every piece of litter; we scoured the gutters. We even peered into litter bins outside shops.

'It probably wasn't along here you lost it,' said Hatty, after a while. 'Wouldn't it have happened when you were running?'

She was right. And then I had a sudden inspiration.

'I know!' I said. 'By the park. I tripped over the kerb and nearly went flying. Maybe it's there.'

I glanced at my watch. We had to be careful; if we were late home from school we'd have some explaining to do. When I saw the time, I was appalled.

'Come on, Hatty!' I said, breaking into a painful jog. 'School finished five minutes ago. There'll be loads of kids at the park!'

She knew what I meant. There are gangs of kids who hardly seem to spend any time at home at all. They just hang around the streets and the park for hours. Mansoor's like that. The moment he gets home, he's sent out again with his little sisters.

We could see the park gates in the distance, and I think I could have won an Olympic Gold with the sprint I did when I saw what was happening.

A little girl was crouched on the ground, examining something curiously. I knew exactly what it was. There wasn't time to think about the crowd of bigger kids who were laughing and jostling each other, a little way behind her. I just ran up, grabbed her wrist and squeezed hard, so that she dropped Cyberpest to the floor. Snatching it up, I turned to run. The little girl burst into tears but I didn't care.

'Hey!' shouted a voice behind me. 'Come back! What d'you think you're doing to my sister?'

I fled. I knew that voice only too well. It was Mansoor.

1∅

Found!

There was no chance. Mansoor is a brilliant runner and was fresh and furious. He got me before the end of the street.

Grabbing my shoulder, he swung me round.

'Rob!' he gasped, his face a mixture of anger and complete shock.

'Sorry!' I pleaded. 'I didn't mean to make her cry. It's just...'

Hatty came panting up behind us and finished my sentence for me. 'It's just we're having a really awful time.'

Mansoor looked bewildered. 'You weren't in school today. What are you doing here? I don't get it. What was it...?'

He looked down at my clenched fist.

'What did you snatch off Firzhana?'

'Show him,' said Hatty. 'Tell him.' She had always liked Mansoor.

I didn't need to. At that moment, Cyberpest began to shriek.

'Not that old cyberpet!' exclaimed Mansoor. 'I don't believe it!'

'It's not just an ordinary cyberpet,' I said

desperately. 'Look, we've got to go home or we're going to get in a terrible row. Could you come round to our house later?'

'I'm not sure.' Mansoor looked like he was making a rapid calculation. 'I've got to look after the girls until supper—but I might be able to get away. It'd better be a good explanation, though, or I'll kill you.'

He would as well. Mansoor is very protective of his little sisters. 'It is, I promise. Please try,' I said. Suddenly, the secret of Cyberpest was too much. I wanted to tell someone else.

'I'll do my best,' he promised and began running back to Firzhana.

'Come on!' I said to Hatty, when I'd talked Cyberpest into shutting up. 'We're late. We'll have to run.'

'I can't,' said Hatty obstinately. 'I've got a stitch and my legs feel like lead.'

'Oh, Hat. Come on. You can do it,' I urged.

'No. I shall just pray that Mum is back late tonight.'

I groaned. 'Oh Hatty. You and your prayers. You really believe there's someone up there listening, don't you?'

'It works,' she said stubbornly. 'I prayed about the security man. And I prayed you wouldn't get run over earlier. I'm always praying, actually.'

'Huh,' I grunted. 'A fat lot of good it's done

us today. It's been a disaster.'

'No, it hasn't! We didn't get arrested. You didn't get splatted. The man didn't catch us. The woman gave up on us. Mansoor didn't beat you up.'

She had a point. 'And you prayed about all those things?'

'Of course.' She looked smug.

I felt like kicking her.

'Oh yeah?' I said. 'So you just pray for what you want and it happens, does it? God's like some super Santa Claus, just doling out goodies whenever you want them? Even if you haven't been good?'

'Don't be stupid, Rob. It depends what you pray for. You can't just pray for a new bike or something. You've got to pray for the right things. Well, I think that's how it works...' She was looking worried.

'Ha!' I said triumphantly. 'Ha! Explain this then. Why does God keep answering your prayers when all day we've been telling lies? I thought lying was supposed to be wrong.'

'But we were only trying to look after Cyberpest,' said Hatty uncertainly.

'And that makes skiving school and pretending I'm a girl all right?'

'I don't know. But it's got to be better than leaving Cyberpest at home to die.'

We walked on in silence. I couldn't be

bothered to argue any more. I was so tired with all that running and the excitement, that I couldn't wait to collapse in front of the TV—but my brain was still churning through the day's events.

Hatty was right. We'd had an amazing number of lucky escapes. Lucky? Was that all there was to it? Was there really someone out there helping us? Aliens in cyberpets. Extra-terrestrial powers. This was beginning to sound like 'The X-Files'.

'Hatty,' I said, as we reached the end of our road. 'If there is a God out there, why has he suddenly sent Cyberpest?'

'I don't know,' said Hatty, 'but I'll tell you one thing. Mum isn't back from work yet. Her car isn't in the drive.'

Mum got back five minutes later. She clearly had too much on her mind to notice how droopy we were. ('You see?' I said, smugly, but Rob had his eyes glued to the television and ignored me.)

'Oh, this is such a nuisance!' Mum said, to no one in particular. 'I wanted to get away from work early to go to Tesco's. It'll be jam-packed now—and I heard at the surgery they had a problem with the checkouts today—some joker hacking into the main computer and sending silly messages. I just hope it's sorted out by now.'

I blushed and stared fixedly at the television screen.

'Awh, Mum!' groaned Rob. 'We don't have to come, do we? I'm tired out. And Mansoor said he might come round.'

I was busy praying again. Rob hadn't put me off. Anyway, I liked the idea of God being there to help me far too much. But we simply couldn't go back to the supermarket. What if the security guard spotted us with Mum and decided to say something? And what might Cyberpest do next? But you can never tell with Mum. She's never sure whether we're old enough to be left on our own in the house or not.

She glanced at her watch. 'Well...' she said. 'It would be much easier to go on my own—and your dad should be in before long. When did Mansoor say he would come?'

'He didn't.'

'Oh well. He's a sensible boy. But don't answer the door to anyone else. All right?'

And then she was off. At which moment, the television began to flicker and go fuzzy.

'Oh blow!' said Rob and got up to fiddle with the controls.

But somehow I knew exactly who was causing the problem.

'If that's you messing with the telly, Cyberpest, then cut it out!' I hissed. 'We've had just about enough of you today. There's cars out there just waiting to crush you and don't you forget it.'

Immediately, the television returned to normal,

but to my amazement, Rob switched it off. And Cyberpest began to wail.

'You can't say that!' said Rob, turning on me. 'That's terrible. It's like telling a little kid you're going to kill it, or threatening it with the bogeyman or something. You've really upset it now. Look!'

And he pulled the screaming Cyberpest out of his pocket and thrust it under my nose.

It was sitting at the bottom of the screen, its spikes all quivery and on end, tears pouring down its cheeks.

'Well, it deserves to be upset,' I said crossly. 'After the day we've had with it.'

'It was only naughty once and that was in Tesco's. The rest was our fault.'

'What about the television just now?'

'It was just being curious. You've got to think of it as a child. It's just trying things out.'

'Ha!' I snapped. 'You've changed your tune. You were the one who wanted to chuck it under a lorry at first!'

'Yes, but not any more. Not once I knew it really was alive. We can't just kill it!'

I knew that, of course. Hadn't I promised to be its mummy? 'Well,' I said grumpily. 'I didn't mean it. And people say far worse things to real kids. And they hit them.'

'Well, they shouldn't,' said Rob firmly. 'And how was Cyberpest supposed to know you didn't mean it? It was only today that you *did* throw it into the road.'

'Well, it probably didn't know what was happening.'

'Oh yeah? Why d'you think it's screaming so much now? I think you'd better say sorry. And be quick about it.'

'Oh, give it here then,' I snapped. Apart from anything else, I couldn't stand that awful din for much longer.

'I'm sorry,' I said, in what was meant to be a soothing voice. 'I didn't mean it. I just keep losing my temper. I didn't mean it about the lorries. And I won't chuck you in the road ever again, OK? I promise.'

The screaming lessened a bit but not a lot and the little alien simply rolled itself into a spiky ball on the floor of its screen. It looked like a multi-coloured, quivering hedgehog.

I tried again. 'Oh, come on, Cyberpest. I've said sorry. I didn't mean it, honestly. It can't be that bad. Is there something else you want? Food? A nice hot drink? Shall we play a game?'

I stroked it despairingly but the noise went on. Rob was there too, murmuring comforting noises. But it wasn't going to forgive me that easily. It was thoroughly upset. I felt awful. The wailing had this dreadful lost, lonely sound. It chilled me to the bone.

I began to cry myself. I was tired and guilty

and my ears were hurting. 'Oh, I'm sorry,' I sobbed. 'I didn't mean it. What are we going to do?'

At that moment the doorbell rang.

11

A New Ally

It was Mansoor.

'Crikey!' he said, covering his ears. 'What's that awful din? Have I set the burglar alarm off, or something?'

'It's Cyberpest,' said Hatty. 'Look.'

Mansoor looked down at the wailing creature in Hatty's hand.

'Wow!' he shouted above the noise. 'I've never seen one as good as that! Where d'you get it?'

It took us a long time to explain, what with the noise and with Mansoor refusing to believe us. By the time we'd convinced him, Cyberpest was wailing in an exhausted, broken way. It was still dreadful but at least it was quieter.

'But now we just don't know what to do to stop it crying. And we'll have to shut it up somehow before Mum gets back,' I said.

'Can I hold it?' asked Mansoor.

Hatty handed it over.

'Poor little thing,' he murmured. (Well, at least, that's what I think he said—it was very difficult to hear anything as my ears were suffering from overload.) 'It must be awful being

so upset and not able to tell anyone what's wrong.'

Hatty snatched Cyberpest back again.

'Mansoor, you're brilliant!' she cried. 'It can *tell us what's wrong. Come on!'*

'Hatty, what are you doing?' I shouted as I followed her up the stairs, two at a time. But with the words still on my lips, I knew.

The computer!

Already, Hatty was in Mum and Dad's bedroom, switching it on. Mum has computer phobia. She thinks computer games are a complete waste of time and that we should be outside doing something more healthy instead. We have to ask to use it and there's none of this inviting your friends round and playing on it for hours. So Hatty was breaking all the rules. But she had to do it.

We stared at the blank screen. It was ready to create a new file.

'Go on,' I urged, as Hatty paused and looked nervous. 'Ask Cyberpest something. Anything. Quick, before my eardrums burst!'

'What if it doesn't work?'

'Oh, just do it, Hatty. Here, let me try.'

I took a deep breath. 'Tell us what's wrong, Cyberpest,' I said.

The screen flickered. A stream of multi-coloured gibberish flashed past. I gripped Hatty's arm so hard that she yelped. And then, in rainbow-coloured letters, just like at the supermarket, a message appeared.

I want to go home.

'Oh no!' I groaned. 'It's ET all over again!'

'Where is home?' asked Hatty eagerly.

I don't know.

And then the wailing, which had stopped, began all over again.

'Please don't cry,' I said gently. 'You've no idea how it hurts our ears.'

Cyberpest made obvious efforts to calm down.

You never told me that before. You just shout at me. And ask me if I want more food.

It was pitiful. And Cyberpest was right. We'd never bothered to explain anything to it. We had just tried to keep it quiet. It wasn't surprising it wanted to go home. If it ever could.

Hatty began to cry again. 'I'm sorry, Cyberpest,' she sobbed. 'I didn't think. I've been an awful mummy.'

'Me too,' I croaked. 'An awful dad, I mean. Sorry, Cyberpest. Things'll be different from now on. We promise.'

I felt dreadful. We had never considered Cyberpest's feelings at all. We'd just tried to keep it quiet with food and games and stuff.

Mansoor was standing gaping at the screen as if he couldn't believe his eyes.

'This is incredible,' he said. 'Is this really happening?'

'You bet it is,' said Hatty, grimly, with a loud sniff. 'How d'you feel about being Cyberpest's uncle?'

'You're on,' said Mansoor, his eyes lighting up.

'You're lucky it's grown up a bit,' I said. 'It was dreadful while it was a baby.'

'What? Worse than this?'

'Definitely,' said Hatty.

Cyberpest made a funny little noise and I peered at it. It had unrolled and was yawning and rubbing its eyes.

'You look like you need to go to sleep,' I said comfortingly. 'You snuggle down now. It'll all be a lot better in the morning.'

And I was rewarded by the screen going blank.

'Oh, gross,' said Mansoor, struggling to keep his face straight. 'You sound like my mum when Firzhana's had a bad dream.'

'You dare laugh,' I said fiercely. 'If you're going to be Cyberpest's uncle, you'd just better not make the same stupid mistakes we've made. You talk to it nicely or else!'

'Ooh, I'm shaking,' said Mansoor, with a grin.

'I mean it,' I snapped.

'Keep your hair on, Rob,' he said. 'I was only joking. It's incredible. I feel like I'm on another planet. But I'll have to go. I left the little ones with Rasheed—and Mum'll skin me if she finds out. Can I come round sometime on Sunday?

We're out all day tomorrow.'

'In the afternoon,' I said. 'We've got church in the morning.'

Mansoor pulled a face. 'That's nearly two days before I see that thing again. I can hardly wait.'

'Don't call it a "thing",' said Hatty crossly, shutting down the computer. 'I know it's asleep but perhaps it can hear you.'

'There's a thought,' I said as we walked downstairs. 'We'll have to be much more careful about what we say. We've probably been hurting its feelings terribly. Perhaps we'd better stop calling it Cyberpest. How about just CP?'

12

It's a Nightmare!

I got up the next morning, feeling better than I had done for days. Cyberpest had slept all night. Perhaps it was exhausted after all the trouble it had caused. A week's holiday stretched ahead of us. And Mansoor was going to help. Best of all, Cyberpest could talk to us! Surely that would make things easier?

One thing was still bugging me. Cyberpest would be much older by the end of the week, but we were still going to have to take it to school. And even a five-year-old would need a lot of entertaining. I mean, it wasn't just going to sit there all day, was it? A whole week to attend to its every need—but what then? It was still going to starve to death if we left it at home and I didn't fancy skiving ever again.

Cyberpest bleeped loudly.

'Food, CP?' I asked contentedly. It was great not having to leap out of bed and get ready for school. 'A nice drink of orange juice?'

But Cyberpest had other ideas. The bleeping continued. This wasn't right. It always wanted food and a drink first thing in the morning.

Maybe I shouldn't have mentioned orange juice.

'Don't you want orange?' I asked. 'How about apple juice instead?'

But the bleeping continued. 'Water?' I suggested. 'Milk? Tea? Coffee? Hot Chocolate?'

But it didn't quieten down. What was the matter with it?

'Look, CP,' I said, patiently. 'Those are the only drinks I can think of for breakfast. You'll have to choose one of them.'

Choose? Of course! What was I doing, lying in bed throwing ideas at it? It could *tell* me what it wanted now! I just had to go and switch on the computer.

Which was when I realized that we had another problem. You don't just switch on the computer in our house. You have to get permission. And you don't get it very often.

I jumped out of bed and stuffed Cyberpest under my pillow.

'I'll be back in a minute,' I told it. 'And then we can sort out breakfast. Right now I've got to talk to Rob. Please try to be quiet. Just for a little while.'

But it didn't shut up. Let's face it, it was still only about two years old.

Rob was not pleased to be woken.

'Oh, go away, Hat!' he moaned. 'I haven't had much sleep this week.'

'Neither have I!' I snapped. 'And now

Cyberpest's wailing again and won't shut up. I can't go and switch the computer on without asking Mum.'

'Well, go and ask Mum, then, stupid.'

'Stupid yourself. She's going to say yes is she, when I'm not dressed and I haven't had breakfast or cleaned my teeth or anything?'

'Well, what're you talking to me about it for, then?' said Rob grumpily. 'Just get yourself sorted out!'

I felt like hitting him.

'Sometimes you are really dense,' I told him. 'It's wailing *now*! And you know what Mum's like. If I go on the computer now, she'll spend the rest of the day telling me I've already had my go. *You'll* have to go on the computer while I go down and pretend you're still fast asleep.'

'Oh no!' groaned Rob, pushing back his duvet reluctantly. 'Not more lies. Not after what happened yesterday.'

'Well, whose fault was that?' I snapped. 'It was your idea to skive off school.'

'Yeah, and it was a mistake, all right?'

'So are you going on the computer or not? I haven't got all day!' I was nearly jumping up and down with impatience.

He pulled a sweatshirt on over his pyjamas.

'Oh, I suppose so,' he said huffily. 'I can't think of a better plan. *You're* the one that talks to God.'

I crept into Mum and Dad's room with Cyberpest wrapped in a jumper and clutched to my chest. It didn't do much to deaden the noise. By the time I'd got the blank screen in front of me, I was sweating.

'What's the matter then, CP? Why are you wailing?' I asked.

Multi-coloured gibberish raced across the screen. And then…

I want to choose my own breakfast.

'Well, that's easy,' I said. 'Go on. Say what you want.'

I don't know what it's called.

Oh great! Of the millions of different foods in the world, which should I start with? But something must have brought on this strange demand. Cyberpest had been quite happy with 'food' and 'drink' until now. Why this sudden fussiness?

Then I had an inspiration.

'Did you see it at the supermarket yesterday?' I asked.

Yes. A lady was giving it to people.

Phew! I wished Hatty was here so she could see what a genius I was.

'You mean waffles,' I said delightedly. 'The lady was giving out samples of some new waffles. OK?'

And I want a drink.

'OK,' I said, very pleased with myself and

oozing confidence. 'What d'you want to drink?'

Coca-Cola.

'Oh no,' I said. 'Sorry. You can't have Coca-Cola for breakfast. It's not a healthy drink. Choose something else.'

But I want Coca-Cola.

'Sorry, not for breakfast. You can have some later on.'

I want Coca-Cola. I want Coca-Cola.

'Look,' I said firmly. 'If you carry on like that, I shall just turn off the screen. And you don't say "I want". You say, "Please may I have...?" OK?'

More multi-coloured gibberish and then Cyberpest began the most abominable shrieking I have ever heard.

'Stop it!' I yelled. 'Stop that this minute. If you don't stop it, I'll...'

I'll what? Chuck you under a car? Give you a good shaking? Stamp up and down on you? I couldn't say any of those, not after the hard time I'd given Hatty yesterday. Apart from the fact that it would be wrong. I shoved my fingers in my ears and tried to think calmly.

'Robert!' It was Mum shouting from the hall. I could only just hear her. 'What on earth are you doing up there? What's that dreadful row?'

'Sorry!' I bellowed. 'It's my old cyberpet! There's something wrong with it. I'll have it fixed in a minute!'

'Take the battery out, for goodness' sake,

then,' shouted Mum. 'It's unbearable!'

'Just you listen here,' I yelled at Cyberpest. 'Be quiet. Now. I mean it. We can't keep you in this house, if you behave like this. And there's no more breakfast until you co-operate. Got it?'

The quiet was deafening. I cupped my ears and rocked my head gently from side to side.

'Uh,' I said accusingly. 'Don't you dare do that again. It hurt!'

Hatty tapped me on the shoulder. 'Crikey, Rob,' she said. 'What was all that about?'

Briefly, I explained what had happened. 'It's a nightmare,' I said. 'What if we have to go through that every mealtime?'

Hatty shrugged. 'But why not let it have Coca-Cola? Just because it's bad for us, it doesn't mean it's bad for aliens. Maybe they like sugar and acid.'

I hadn't thought of that. 'But now I've said it can't,' I wailed. 'I'll look like a real jerk if I change my mind.'

'Ssh,' said Hatty. 'I bet it's listening.'

I glanced at the tiny screen. Cyberpest was huddled up in a corner, all droopy spikes. I would have felt sorry for it, if my ears hadn't still been ringing.

'Listen,' I said, in a voice that sounded uncomfortably like Dad's when he's being very serious with me. 'Hatty and I are going to have to discuss your behaviour. You are to stay in

Hatty's room and keep quiet until we are ready. And then we'll talk breakfast.'

Cyberpest didn't reply. I turned off the computer. I had thought things would be easier now that he could talk. Some hope!

13

A Fight

'Well?' said Hatty. 'What now? Are we going to let it have some Coke or not?'

I shrugged. 'Dunno. I don't want to give in just because it threw a tantrum.'

Hatty giggled. 'Oh dear,' she said. 'You sound terribly grown-up.'

'Well, we're going to have to be grown-up,' I said, impatiently. 'If we don't watch out we're going to have a spoilt brat of a Cyberpest on our hands. And I don't fancy that, thank you very much!'

'Keep your hair on, Rob,' said Hatty. 'It's never had a tantrum before. And it's done what you told it to do now.'

I snorted. 'But we still don't know what to do about its breakfast. And all its other meals! What are we going to do? Sit there listing every food we can think of until we come up with what it wants? Remembering the waffles was just luck. I could have been sitting here all morning. I could...'

'Oh, you do go on,' said Hatty. 'Why don't you stop panicking and let me say something?'

'Go on, then,' I said grumpily. 'Say something, Einstein.'

She smiled sweetly. 'Well, the first thing is that we don't want it thinking it can trample all over us. But, on the other hand, we do have to take account of its feelings.'

'Yes, oh great one,' I muttered.

'Shut up. We have a choice. Either we just tell it what it can have for each meal and say, "Like it or lump it"...'

'Like Mum does...'

'Yes. Or we can explain to it that, seeing as we don't really know what an alien should eat, it can choose what it wants. It has to look after itself.'

'Now you sound like our Head,' I objected. 'And CP is only about two years old!'

'Huh!' said Hatty darkly. 'It's a bit advanced for a two-year-old if you ask me. How many toddlers do you know that can write? And spell?'

She had a point.

'You mean, not only does it get older quicker, it's developing faster than we do too?' I asked. 'But two-year-olds do have tantrums.'

'Human ones do. When their parents ignore them. Especially in supermarkets. When they want sweets.'

Of course! That little kid screaming at the checkout, just before Cyberpest's message appeared on the screen!

'You mean CP pretended to have a tantrum? Just to get its own way?'

'That's right.'

It was a daunting thought. The little brain inside that screen was more than a match for ours. And Hatty's was more than a match for mine.

'This is getting too weird for me,' I said. 'I don't think I can cope.'

'It wants to go home,' said Hatty. 'So let's try to help.'

Easier said than done. I had my breakfast and then secretly we went to talk to Cyberpest.

'OK,' said Hatty, picking it up. 'You can stop pretending you're asleep. We know that tantrum wasn't for real. You just copied it off that kid in the supermarket. If you want our help to get you home, you'd better start being honest with us. We never asked you to come and live with us and we're doing our best—but you're not exactly co-operative.'

Please may I have some Coca-Cola.

'You do have a one-track mind.'

No. I have a multi-track mind. That is my big advantage over you.

'OK. It was a stupid thing to say. But you don't have much sense of humour.'

Agreed. Now please may I have some Coca-Cola ?

I sighed. 'Look, we've been thinking about it.

Coke is really bad for humans and we wouldn't be allowed to have it for breakfast. But we don't know what aliens like you should eat—so if you want to, go on. Have some Coca-Cola.'

Thank you.

Well, at least it was learning some manners.

'Rob! Hatty! What are you doing up there?' It was Mum.

'Oh—er—nothing much,' I called back.

'Well, come down then. It's a beautiful day. Let's go for a bike ride.'

We all enjoyed being out on our bikes—even Cyberpest. The next problem was its lunch. Mum only lets us on the computer for about a quarter of an hour at a time. Any more than that and she thinks we'll turn into zombies. Were we going to have to spend all our time letting Cyberpest choose its food? And what were we going to do once we were back at school?

Rob wolfed his lunch and then asked if he could go on the computer.

'Fine,' said Mum. 'But only for fifteen minutes, remember.'

I was more sedate. Mum had made a sticky gingerbread and I was savouring every mouthful. I wasn't that desperate to talk to Cyberpest.

But when I went up to the computer, I couldn't believe it! Rob was playing a stupid arcade game!

'Rob!' I hissed. 'What on earth are you doing?

Why aren't you talking to CP?'

'Oh, I've given it lunch,' he said casually. 'I just tried all the junk food. It was easy. More Coke, a Mars Bar and a packet of Pringles.'

'Ugh,' I said. 'Not exactly very healthy.'

Rob shrugged, his hand still on the mouse.

'You were the one that said...'

'Oh, never mind that now,' I interrupted. 'Why aren't you still talking to it?'

'What?' Rob's eyes were glued to the screen. I might as well have been talking to a brick wall.

'Why aren't you talking to it? Don't you remember? You're doing just what it doesn't like. Feeding it and then ignoring it unless it cries.'

'Well, it isn't crying.'

'Neither am I but that doesn't mean I want you to ignore me.'

Rob's hand moved feverishly on the mouse.

'I said, "that doesn't mean I want you to ignore me."'

'What? Can't you be quiet, Hatty? I'm trying to concentrate!'

That did it. I reached out for the off button.

But Rob was too quick for me. Quick as a flash, he pushed me aside.

'Don't you dare!' he shouted. 'You know very well you can't just switch off! You have to shut it down properly. And it's my go and if I want to play a game, then I will. You talk to CP if you want to, when it's your turn!'

I lost my temper.

'You idiot!' I screamed, trying to drag him off the typing chair. 'It wants to go home! How are we ever going to find out how to send it if you won't talk to it? We hardly get any time on the computer—and you're playing stupid games!'

Rob gets very aggressive when he's been on the computer. That's another reason Mum doesn't like us using it very much. He thumped me in the stomach and I grabbed him round the neck, so he finally got off the typing chair and threw me on the floor. When Mum came in, we were rolling around, kicking, scratching and tearing at each other's clothes. And Cyberpest, who was lying by the computer, was wailing fit to waken the dead.

'Rob! Hatty! Stop that this minute! And turn that wretched cyberpet off!' she shouted, pulling us apart.

I staggered to my feet, panting, and snatched up Cyberpest.

'I'm going to my room,' I announced and stalked out.

'Don't think you can get away with this, young lady,' called Mum, as I slammed my door. 'I shall be speaking to you shortly.' That was OK. Rob would get the worst of it. And he deserved it.

That's not fair.

Oh yes it is.

No it isn't. Don't start on at me again. I admitted I was wrong didn't I? And I said I was sorry. And it wasn't as bad as threatening to chuck CP under a lorry.

Now who's going on?

You started it. Look, I think I should write this bit.

Why?

Because I want to. It was mainly my fault.

Oh, all right. Go on then.

Mum went ballistic. I was absolutely furious with Hatty for leaving me to face her on my own, even though I knew she'd only done it because of Cyberpest. She's not a bad kid, really.

Thanks a lot.

Oh, shut up and let me get on, will you?

Anyway, you can guess what happened. If that was what being allowed on the computer did to us and if that was how we were going to behave near it etc. etc. then we weren't going to be allowed to use it—not for three whole days.

I begged. I pleaded. I even cried. Mum was

not impressed. She just told me to stop snivelling and grow up. I dreaded to think what Hatty would say when I told her—but Mum saved me the bother. As soon as she'd finished with me, she went and started on Hat.

Ten minutes later, I crept into Hatty's room. She was sitting on her bed, talking to Cyberpest, explaining what had happened.

'Sorry, Hat,' I said. 'You were right. Sorry, CP. I've really blown it now.'

'Only for three days,' said Hatty. 'And it was my fault too. I think CP understands. Look!'

I gazed down at the little, black screen. Cyberpest wasn't angry or upset. He looked a bit bumpy but he hadn't grown any spikes and his face just looked a bit fed-up.

'We have to talk to him,' said Hatty.

'Him?'

'I'm sure he's a him. And we can't just keep calling him "it".'

'Well, in three days, we can ask him,' I said gloomily.

'Yes, and loads of other things too. We have to think about what he wants—not just about what we want all the time.'

'OK, OK. Thanks for the lecture. I get the message. I just don't think I'm cut out to be a dad yet, that's all.'

14

An Offer We Couldn't Refuse?

The next day was Sunday—and I'd hardly crawled out of bed before Mansoor arrived.

'You're early,' I said, as I opened the door. 'I thought I said come in the afternoon. We've got church soon.'

'Couldn't wait any longer,' he replied. 'D'you have to go to church? Dad always goes to the mosque on Fridays but us kids don't have to bother.'

I shrugged. I never knew what to say when Mansoor started talking about his family's religion. Occasionally, I'd tried to explain a bit about church—but he always looked at me as if I was out of my tree. Hatty's much better at that sort of thing—it means more to her.

Anyway, right then wasn't the time for a chat about God. Mansoor was far too interested in Cyberpest.

'Well? How's he getting on? Have you talked to him much? What have you found out?'

'Not a lot. We haven't had chance. Bit of a disaster yesterday, I'm afraid...'

And I explained what had happened.

'What did you do about giving him his tea then?' demanded Mansoor.

'Oh, that was easy enough. He had chicken nuggets and chips and ice-cream. He loves junk food. We just kept listing things until he looked cheerful. I think the meals will be OK—it's just that we want him to talk back—then we might be able to help him get home.'

'Well, bring him round to my house,' said Mansoor. 'I'm allowed on the computer any time I want—unless I'm doing a job for my mum. In fact, you might as well let me look after him while you go to church. It'll save you a lot of bother.'

I should have been grateful, shouldn't I? Someone asking to babysit for nothing? But, suddenly, I didn't want to let go. Cyberpest was ours—mine and Hatty's. Much as I liked Mansoor, I didn't want to hand Cyberpest over and just go and leave him. And I had this sudden, awful feeling that once I handed him over, it would be very hard to get him back. I mean, Mansoor has a computer he can play on almost whenever he likes. It would make much more sense for Mansoor to keep Cyberpest all the time. He might even prefer living at Mansoor's house and cry when he came home to us—if he ever did. I couldn't stand that—not any of it. Weird, wasn't it?

Something else was bugging me too. There had to be a reason for Cyberpest suddenly appearing in our lives. I was sure of it. Call me a loony if you like, but I had the feeling that Cyberpest had been sent specially for us. That however hard it was, we had to keep him. Perhaps all Hatty's God-talk had been getting to me.

It took about five seconds for all that to pass through my mind.

'No thanks,' I said promptly. 'I'll bring CP round this afternoon but I think he ought to come to church with us. He hasn't had time to get used to you yet.'

'He could get used to me now,' wheedled Mansoor. 'Where is he?'

'With Hatty. She had him overnight. He usually wakes up quite a bit and wants stories and snacks. I'd better not disturb her.' I began to close the door. 'I'll have to go now. I've got to clean my shoes. But we'll be round this afternoon, I promise.'

'Oh, OK then,' said Mansoor, disappointed. He turned away. 'See you later.'

I shut the door and leaned against it with a huge sigh of relief. Phew! That had been close. I felt very odd and slightly shaky.

I went to find Hatty. She was sitting up in bed, singing to Cyberpest.

'Does he like that?' I asked curiously.

''Course he does,' she said, a big grin on her face. 'Look. He's dancing!'

Sure enough, he was.

'Hey, CP, you're quite a dancer!' I said. 'We'll have to put a tape on.'

'Excuse me,' said Hatty, offended. 'What's wrong with my singing?'

'Nothing. But I want to talk to you.'

We found a tape and when Cyberpest was happily boogying along to it, I told Hatty about Mansoor's offer.

'You didn't say yes, did you?' demanded Hatty.

'No—but I felt really weird about it. All sort of jealous—and like he was trying to steal something really precious from me.'

'Well, of course you would—so do I! CP isn't just a toy. He's like our baby.'

'Well, real babies have babysitters.'

'Yes, but I bet their Mums and Dads feel funny about it at first. And they don't just send their babies off with complete strangers.'

'But Mansoor isn't a complete stranger.'

'He is to CP. He needs to get to know him first.'

'Hatty, I don't like this. I never realized it would be so complicated.'

'Well, we'll just have to work very hard at helping CP get home.'

'But that's just it. If I felt all weird about

letting Mansoor babysit for an hour or so, how am I going to feel when CP goes back where he came from?'

Hatty shrugged, helplessly. 'Kids leave home,' she said. 'That's the way it is.'

We sat and thought for a while.

'Hat,' I said, after a few minutes. 'D'you think Mum and Dad feel like this about us?'

'Guess they must,' she agreed. 'Though I can hardly believe it sometimes.'

15

Home Alone

Half an hour later, we were in the car, on our way to church. It was one of those times—those times when it's hard to believe your parents would care tuppence if they never saw you again in their lives. We'd spent the last twenty minutes being yelled at. So I hadn't finished my breakfast. So we hadn't cleaned our teeth. So we hadn't brushed our hair or cleared away our breakfast things. Are these major crimes? Will we die if we don't do them? Anyone would think we'd immediately starve to death, lose all our teeth, sprout head lice and find rats invading the kitchen, the way Mum and Dad go on at us. Why do grown-ups never realize that sometimes—just sometimes—kids have more on their minds than clean bodies and a tidy house?

'I bet we had babysitters when we were only a week old while they went off for a night out,' I said to Rob as we slumped down on the back seat of the car. 'And I bet when we leave home, they'll just say, "Thank goodness. No more Weetabix crumbs to clear up."'

It wasn't until we were half-way to church

that I realized what I'd done.

'Rob!' I gasped, clapping my hand to my mouth. 'I've gone and left CP in the bathroom!'

'Hatty, you idiot! How could you?'

'It was 'cos I was rushing. I haven't got a pocket on this skirt, so I was holding him in my hand. I put him down to clean my teeth and...'

'You left him there.'

'Mum was shouting at me to hurry up because we were late. I just forgot. What are we going to do?' I was frantic. I think I would have opened the car door and leaped out into the traffic if Rob hadn't been there to stop me.

Rob grabbed my arm. 'Calm down, Hat,' he said. 'And don't start crying. He's sure to be all right. He won't starve to death. We won't be gone longer than an hour or so—and he manages fine on three meals a day and a couple of night-time snacks now that he's bigger.'

I relaxed a bit. 'It's funny, that,' I said. 'D'you suppose it's like he's having one meal a day in his time?'

Rob snorted. 'More like one meal every few months, if you ask me. He needs a lot of daytime naps as well. Perhaps where he comes from the days are much shorter, or maybe he hibernates. What was he doing while you were in the bathroom? Was he asleep?'

'Yes—well, he wasn't on the screen anyway.'

'There you are then. Maybe he'll sleep till we

get back and won't even notice we've gone. Don't worry about it. He'll be all right, I'm sure.'

But I still felt dreadful. There we were, refusing to let Mansoor babysit and I'd left poor old Cyberpest all alone in the bathroom. A great mum I was turning out to be!

I prayed about it in church—that Cyberpest would be all right, and that he wouldn't be frightened. But did God care about Cyberpest? Where *had* he come from? And how did God feel about me, after all the lying I'd done in the last two days? Was lying all right if it was in a good cause?

I was getting pretty confused about God. Sometimes I felt absolutely sure he was there, listening to my every word, and other times—well, I just didn't know. And it was no good asking Mum and Dad. They aren't very sure about God themselves. After all, we haven't been going to church all that long. One of Mum's friends got her to go along and I don't think Dad wanted to be left out.

I had to try and sort it out myself. I could have asked Mum's friend, I suppose, but I didn't like to. I mean, what would I say? 'I've been telling a lot of lies recently—will God still answer my prayers?' I'd be too embarrassed.

So all I could do was carry on praying. And hope that God would understand.

We could hear the noise some way from home.

‘Oh dear, someone’s burglar alarm must have jammed,’ said Mum.

It took me a moment to put two and two together. Then I clutched Rob’s arm urgently.

‘What if…?’

He had got there before me. His face was white.

‘Don’t even think about it,’ he groaned.

‘Oh no!’ we both said together, as we rounded the corner into our street.

Outside our house, there was a police car and a whole crowd of our neighbours.

‘What?’ said Dad. ‘I don’t believe it. Why hasn’t Bill gone in with the spare key and turned it off?’

‘He probably has,’ muttered Rob.

‘What was that?’ snapped Dad, as we pulled up.

‘Oh, nothing.’

There was a stir in the crowd as we appeared and Bill, our next-door neighbour, fought his way through.

‘I’m terribly sorry,’ he said. He’s a sweet, nervous old gentleman. ‘I don’t know if I did something wrong, trying to reset the alarm, but I seem to have jammed it up. It’s been driving everyone mad, so I sent for the police. I couldn’t get a reply from the alarm company.’

‘Has there been a break-in?’ asked Mum gently. Poor Bill was shaking like a leaf.

'The police are having a look—but I don't think so. I think it's just a fault.'

I was jumping up and down with impatience. 'Mum! Dad! I know…'

But at that moment a policeman appeared at the front door and Mum and Dad went pushing through the onlookers to speak to him. We followed them.

The policeman looked very relieved to see our parents. 'At last!' he said, shouting above the din. 'I'm sure you'll be able to sort this out. I think the old gentleman pressed the wrong buttons and, frankly, I thought it best not to interfere. Nothing appears to have been tampered with—it's just a question of stopping the alarm.'

Dad looked worried. 'Well, I'll try,' he said. 'It ought to be simple enough. We've never had this problem before.'

I was half-way up the stairs but Mum stopped me.

'Where are you going, Harriet? Stay down here until the police say you can go up. If there has been a break-in, they won't want anything disturbed.'

'But the policeman said…'

'Just do as you're told,' Mum snapped. 'This isn't the time to argue.'

Honestly, parents! The slightest bit of stress and their brains explode. I looked at Rob, despairingly. He rolled his eyes and crossed his legs. I got the message.

'But Mum,' I whined. 'I'm desperate to go to the loo!'

'You're old enough to wait!'

The siren carried on wailing. Dad was having no luck with the code.

'Please, Mum,' I begged. 'Please. I'll burst if I don't go. Ask the policeman if it's all right!'

Fortunately, the policeman had a few brain cells left.

'Oh, she can go up,' he said, smiling at my impression of a cross-legged kangaroo. 'There's no sign of a break-in.'

I raced up the stairs. Cyberpest was lying where I had left him. I picked him up and inspected the screen anxiously. He was very angry and fed up. All his spikes were on end, his arms were folded and he was tapping his foot impatiently. I don't think I've ever seen such a grumpy face.

'I'm so sorry, CP,' I said. 'Mum was going on at me, and I just forgot to pick you up again. Please stop the burglar alarm now. It's driving everyone mad. The police are here, and Bill from next door looks like he's about to have a heart attack. I'm really sorry. I didn't mean it, honestly.'

Cyberpest's spikes quivered. His face looked very grim. For a moment, I thought he wasn't going to co-operate. And then, quite suddenly, he sat down on the floor of his screen and began to cry. The siren stopped. From outside the house, I heard a cheer. In the hall, the grown-ups were congratulating each other and Dad was muttering about faults and darned nuisances and things not being the same nowadays.

I sat on the floor of the bathroom with Cyber-pest and stroked him soothingly.

'I'm sorry,' I kept saying, over and over again. 'I didn't mean to leave you all on your own like that.'

Rob burst into the bathroom and peered over my shoulder. 'Whoops!' he said. 'I think that was a *real* tantrum.'

16

Where Do You Come From?

We thought that as soon as the police had gone, we would beg to go on the computer and be able to talk to Cyberpest. But he went to sleep. Either that or he was choosing to be invisible, giving us a taste of how he'd felt that morning when we'd abandoned him. Anything could happen with Cyberpest. But I think he was asleep, worn out by all the upset and his efforts with the burglar alarm. He missed lunch and the screen was still blank when we left for Mansoor's house.

Hatty was worried. 'What if he doesn't wake up soon? Maybe Mansoor'll think we were playing some sort of trick on him?'

I shrugged. 'He'll wake up,' I said. 'He must be hungry. And Mansoor's seen him. He knows it's not a trick.'

'He didn't see him for very long,' said Hatty.

I must admit things did get pretty tense. By half-past three, when we'd been twiddling our thumbs at Mansoor's house for well over an hour, he was getting impatient. 'Is this some sort of con?' he asked. 'It's not April Fool's Day, you know.'

'But you've seen him,' I said. 'We just have to be patient. He's asleep.'

'Well, why don't you wake him up?'asked Mansoor.

It was a novel idea. We'd never thought of doing that. I suppose we were always quite relieved when he went to sleep; it was less work for us.

'Well, I suppose we could try…' I said hesitantly. I looked across at Hatty.

She looked equally unsure. 'I think he needs to sleep…' she said.

'He's had ages. And he ought to have something to eat.'

'Oh, go on then,' she said. 'I suppose we'd better or we'll run out of time to talk to him. But don't blame me if he's grumpy.'

'Come on, CP,' I said loudly and gave him a little shake. 'It's time to wake up now.'

Nothing. The screen stayed blank.

I tried again, louder.

'Oh, give him to me,' said Hatty impatiently.

'Wake up, CP. We want to talk to you,' she said gently. 'We're here at Mansoor's house and we can use the computer for as long as we want—except we'll have to go home for tea soon. So why don't you wake up and come and talk to us? You know we're really sorry about this morning.'

And, suddenly, there he was, looking slightly

ruffled, but nothing like so upset as he had been earlier.

'How about some lunch first?' said Hatty.

Cyberpest beamed at her. I tell you, she's a lot better at being a mummy than I am at being a dad, even if she did leave him in the bathroom.

When Cyberpest had stuffed himself with chicken and chips, chocolate cake and lemonade, he looked a lot happier.

'We're really sorry we left you behind,' said Hatty.

Stop saying that, *came the reply.* **I know. I'm sorry too.**

You could have knocked me down with a feather. Somehow I hadn't thought that 'sorry' was a word Cyberpest would use. He had always been so tetchy and demanding.

'Why did you do it?' asked Hatty.

I was cross. I thought it would bring you back.

'Of course he would,' I said excitedly. 'Because of the car alarm.' Cyberpest just doesn't miss a thing. Our car alarm is forever going off—and as soon as it does, someone rushes out of the house to deal with it.

'Don't talk about CP as if he isn't here,' snapped Hatty. 'You know how you hate it when Mum and Dad do that. We were at church,' she added. 'We couldn't hear the alarm until we were nearly home again.'

'You won't do it again, will you, CP?' I said anxiously.

No. But don't leave me alone again, please. It's OK for you. There's loads of you here. But there's only one of me and I'm scared.

Hatty looked as if she was going to cry. It was a bit heartbreaking.

'I prayed you wouldn't be frightened,' she said, with a catch in her voice. 'But it didn't work.'

'Ha!' I snorted. 'Did the super Santa in the sky let you down, then?'

'Oh shut up, stupid!' she snapped. 'I wasn't talking to you.'

She turned back to Cyberpest.

'We'd like to help you find your way home,' she said. 'But we don't know how.'

Neither do I.

'Do you know where you come from?' I asked.

No. Why should I? Do you?

'Why, here, of course. England. Europe. The World.'

But how did you get here?

'I was born here,' I said. 'That's what happens with humans.'

So where did you come from?

'I've told you. Here. England. The World.' What was Cyberpest on about?

'Oh, you are thick sometimes, Rob,' said Hatty, with a sigh. Mansoor was nodding in

agreement. I think that's why she likes him. He's the only kid she knows who's as clever as she is.

'CP means what made you be born,' he said. 'And he doesn't mean because your mum and dad wanted a baby—he means why are you here? Why are any of us here? Who sent us?'

A little shiver ran down my spine. It wasn't something I'd ever really thought about. It was simple as far as I was concerned—all about eggs and sperm getting together. Mum's forever telling me. I suppose that's what comes of being a nurse at a doctor's surgery. But I'd never thought about whether we'd been sent *here or* why *we'd been born. I bet Hatty had though, what with her prayers and her talk about God. She probably thinks about it all the time.*

Not *all* the time, Rob. I'm only a kid.

Oh shut up. You make me feel like an idiot.

You said it.

I shall ignore that.

So there you have it. That was what Cyberpest was going on about.

Suppose you hadn't been born here, *he said.* **Suppose you suddenly popped up in a place where you were the only human. There'd be no one else like you. You'd have no idea how you'd got there or**

why. That's what's happened to me. So I want to know where I should be going.

'It's the same for us in a way,' said Hatty thoughtfully. 'I mean, we know we were born here and that's the same for everyone—but how do we know why we're here—or where we're meant to end up?'

'You mean when we die?' I wasn't sure I liked this conversation.

'Yes. I mean, at church they tell us one thing, Mansoor's family think something else—how do we know who's right?'

It was all getting a bit deep for me.

'I know, I know,' I said impatiently. 'But how does all that help? How do we get CP home?'

I don't think we can, *said Cyberpest.* **I think I was sent here.**

Late that night, when Cyberpest was asleep, I crept into Rob's room.

'Are you awake?'

'Mmm.'

'I can't sleep.'

'Neither can I.'

I curled up at the end of his bed under the duvet.

'What are we going to do?' I didn't have to say what about.

'I don't know. Looks like we're stuck with CP for the rest of our lives.'

'But we can't be! I mean, waking up to give him snacks and tell stories is all very well for now—but not for ever! What about when we're grown-up? What if we get married?'

'Maybe he'll grow out of it.'

'No, it's not like that. It's something to do with his days and nights being different.'

'Well, he's growing up fast. By then he'll be very old. Maybe he'll have…'

'Died? But he might be the sort of creature who lives for hundreds of years!'

'Oh, you're cheerful, aren't you? I'd just worked out that after 210 days he'd be about ready to go to Cyberpest heaven!'

'D'you think there is one?'

'Oh, I don't know, Hatty. I'm not even sure there's a human heaven. You're the one that's into all that stuff.'

We sat in silence for a while, thinking about it. It was dreadful. Only that morning we'd been jealous because Mansoor offered to look after Cyberpest for an hour or so. Now we were counting the days till he died.

'It's the thought of being stuck with him for life,' said Rob. 'I mean, human kids grow up and go away.'

'Not all of them.'

'Most of them.'

'I can't bear it,' I said. 'I mean, I can't bear the thought of not having CP any more but I can’t bear the thought of being stuck with him for the rest of my life, either. What are we going to do?’

‘Over to you, Hatty,’ said Rob. ‘You’d better try praying.’

17

Crisis!

Cyberpest didn't wake that night. When I woke up in the morning, it was a few moments before I realized I hadn't been disturbed. It didn't bother me. Cyberpest had slept all night on Friday too, after all the trouble in Tesco's. Perhaps messing about with computers wore him out.

When there was still no sound out of him after I was dressed and had eaten my breakfast, I was more worried. I asked Rob what he thought. He shrugged.

'Probably just exhausted,' he said. 'Give him another half an hour.'

'And then what?'

'Wake him up, of course.'

The half-hour passed very slowly. Every few minutes I peered at the screen. The trouble was, I wasn't sure it was entirely black. There seemed to be a faint, greenish glow in the middle. But it could have been that my eyes were going funny with staring at it so much.

'He hasn't woken up,' I told Rob at last.

'So? Talk to him then.'

'He's in my room.'

'Well, go and get him! What's the matter with you?'

'I'm worried. What if he kind of sensed what we were saying last night? What if he's gone?'

'He can't have,' said Rob. 'He can't hear us in another room.'

But we both knew we couldn't be certain of that. Rob followed me into my bedroom.

We did our best to wake him. We talked; we shouted; we shook. I even tried singing. Nothing.

'Hatty, is it me or is there a faint sort of glow in the middle of the screen?' said Rob at last.

'It isn't you,' I said slowly. 'I think it's CP. You don't think... you don't think he's sort of fading out, do you?' I couldn't bring myself to say the word 'dying'.

Rob obviously did. 'Come on, CP,' he said urgently. 'Don't fade on us! Make an effort. Tell us what's wrong!'

'He can't, idiot!' I said, but Rob was already yelling down the stairs.

'Mum, can we play on the computer, please?'

'All right—but not for long. Don't forget we're going out to get your new shoes soon!'

Phew! She'd forgotten the three-day ban. We raced into Mum and Dad's bedroom. Why do computers always seem to take so long to start up? I was ready to kick it by the time we had a blank screen.

'What is it?' I said. 'What's wrong, CP?

Please tell us! Have we upset you?'

For a moment, the screen stayed blank. And then, in very faint, green writing, there appeared one word.

Ill.

'Medicine,' said Rob promptly. 'Nurses, doctors, hospitals, operations, X-rays, injections, blood-tests…'

'Robert!' I yelled. 'Shut up! We need to think.'

'But…'

'I tried all that the very first night when I made him sick. All he needed was a clean up and his mummy.'

'Clean up,' said Rob. 'Mummy.'

Sometimes I wonder about my brother. I know he's supposed to be older than me but it's hard to believe at times.

There's no need to be rude. I was panicking.

I noticed.

Oh shut up and get on with the story.

I was doing. It was you that interrupted.

It was you that was rude,

All right, I'm sorry. Will that do?

I suppose it'll have to.

It was at that moment that the doorbell rang.

We ignored it—until we realized that it was Mansoor and that Mum was sending him away because we were about to go shopping. I dashed out onto the landing.

'Mum!' I shouted. 'Call him back. We need to speak to him for a minute.'

'What happened to the word "please", Hatty?'

I ran down the stairs and pushed past Mum.

'Mansoor! We need you! Come back!' I yelled.

'Harriet!' Mum was seriously cross and grabbed me by the arm.

'Upstairs,' I told Mansoor, who wasn't sure if he dared set foot in the house. 'On the computer.'

'Is that OK...?' Mansoor looked at Mum.

'Oh, go on, then,' said Mum irritably. 'But you, young lady, can stay here and explain what you mean by being so rude.'

'I'm sorry,' I said. 'I was in a hurry. I didn't mean it. I won't do it again. Can I go now? Please?'

Mum looked at me, a worried frown on her face.

'I don't know,' she said. 'There's something very funny about you and Rob this last week or so.' But she let me go.

'You'll have to take him home with you,' Rob was saying to Mansoor. 'See if you can find out what's wrong. Perhaps he'll manage to say something else that'll give us a clue.'

‘But...’ For a moment, a great flood of jealousy surged through me. I was beginning to shake.

‘Don’t argue, Hatty. We’re just lucky Mansoor turned up right now. If we had to take CP to the shoe shop, he’d probably be dead by the time we got back!’

‘But can’t we put Mum off somehow? Say we feel sick or something?’

‘There’s no point. She wouldn’t let us play on the computer much longer anyway.’

He was right. And anyway, what was wrong with me? Only last night, I’d been whingeing about being stuck with Cyberpest for the rest of my life. My feelings just wouldn’t behave themselves. My life had been turned upside down. I was confused about everything. Nothing seemed quite the same any more. I took Cyberpest from Rob and stroked him.

‘Come on, CP,’ I whispered. ‘You can do it. We can’t stay with you, but we’ll be back soon and Mansoor’s going to do everything he can to find out what’s wrong. And I’ll pray that you’ll be OK.’

A tear trickled off the end of my nose and splashed onto the screen. I wiped it away with my cuff. Then I held Cyberpest very close to my mouth.

‘I love you, CP,’ I whispered and kissed the screen.

The boys were staring at me, open-mouthed.

They weren't looking at the computer-screen. They didn't see the very, very faint, green writing which flashed up for a split second. But I did.

I love you too, Hatty, it said.

18

Mansoor to the Rescue

We had never been less interested in buying shoes in our lives. Mum couldn't believe how quick we were.

'Are you sure they fit properly?' she kept asking. 'Are you sure you like them?'

I think we had just about enough sense to make sure they were comfortable but that was all. They could have been wellington boots for all we cared.

'Can you drop us off at Mansoor's house?' I demanded, as soon as we were back in the car.

'Honestly,' said Mum. 'I don't know why I went to all that trouble to arrange time off work for your holidays. I might as well have sent you to live with Mansoor for a week!'

'But can you drop us off?'

'No, of course not. It's nearly lunch-time. You can go round later.'

We hardly ate. Mum was cross.

'If this is all about playing some stupid game on Mansoor's computer, I shall stop you from going round there so much,' she said. 'You were there all afternoon yesterday. You don't have

school holidays so you can spend all your time staring at a computer.'

'It's not that, Mum, honestly,' said Hatty. 'Please can we go now?'

'What's come over you, Hatty? I thought Mansoor was Rob's friend. Don't you want any of your friends round here while the boys are out of the way?'

'Tomorrow,' said Hatty. 'I'll have someone round tomorrow.'

And we made our escape.

We arrived at Mansoor's panting and in pain—we had run so fast. Hatty was nearly bent double. But it was worth it.

'It's all right!' Mansoor beamed at us, as he opened the door. 'He's going to be all right! Come and see!'

We nearly pushed Mansoor over in our hurry.

Cyberpest was lying by the computer where Mansoor had left him. We both reached out to snatch him up and then stopped. Was it safe to disturb him?

'It's OK,' said Mansoor. 'Really it is.'

We peered at the screen together. Hatty was gripping my arm so hard that I yelped. But Mansoor was right. Huddled up at the bottom of his screen, looking very tired and droopy and green, lay Cyberpest.

'CP!' breathed Hatty. 'You're going to be all right!'

The computer stayed blank but Cyberpest nodded his head ever so slightly and gave us the faintest glimmer of a multi-coloured smile.

'It was his diet,' said Mansoor proudly. 'I suddenly worked it out.'

'What?' I had been too relieved to see Cyberpest again to question how he'd got better.

'It was dreadful,' said Mansoor. 'By the time I got home, I had to screw up my eyes to see the glow and even then I couldn't be sure I wasn't imagining it. First I talked about every possible treatment I could think of for people that were ill. Then I got the first aid book out and read out the bit about the kiss of life and what to do if someone has a heart attack. Then I tried bathing him with cold water. I even tried putting a thermometer in the bit where his battery ought to be.'

We stared at him in astonishment.

'Well what would you have done? Here I was, stuck with this dying alien that I'd hardly met before, knowing you'd go demented if you got back and he'd gone and died on me. It was terrible.'

I suddenly realized what an awful thing we'd done to Mansoor.

'Sorry,' I said. 'I'm really sorry. But we didn't have much time to think about it.'

'We wouldn't have blamed you if he'd died,' said Hatty. 'It wouldn't have been your fault.'

'Huh!' grunted Mansoor. 'Anyway, none of it helped. It wasn't until lunch-time that I suddenly guessed what might be wrong.'

'Why? What happened then?'

'Mum was yelling at me to come down and I was wondering what on earth I was going to do when I realized that CP probably hadn't eaten all day. I was just thinking that I probably ought to try to feed him when it came to me.'

'What did?'

'That it was his food, of course.'

'His food? What d'you mean?'

'He'd probably been eating the wrong stuff. You'd just been letting him choose what he wanted—and maybe it was really bad for him.'

'Of course!' said Hatty. 'You're a genius, Mansoor.' And she flung her arms round him.

'So what did you do?' I demanded.

'I told him that he might not like it, but he was going to have to drink loads of water. I reckoned that would be as good a start as any.'

'And did he?'

'Well, not at first. Then I remembered what Mum says when I've been sick. "Just one sip at a time," I told him.'

'And what happened?'

'Nothing. And Mum was yelling up the stairs because I hadn't come down for lunch. So I left him to it.'

'You what?'

'I left him to it. There was nothing else I could do. I reckoned I'd just have to wait and see if it worked. I put him in my pocket and went down. It was awful. Mum kept asking me if I was ill or something 'cos I barely touched my food—but when I got him back upstairs, I knew it was going to be all right.'

'How?'

'The glow was brighter. And he's been getting better ever since. I just sat here, telling him to keep drinking water and suddenly, about twenty minutes ago, he re-appeared. I could have kissed him.'

Hatty did kiss him. 'Keep drinking the water,' she told him. 'It's making you better.'

All that afternoon, we hovered around Cyberpest. He got brighter but he still looked terrible. Was he really getting better? Then, just when we were wondering whether to leave him with Mansoor for the night, a faint green message appeared on the computer screen.

I'm hungry, *it said.*

'Great!' I said. 'You must be getting better.'

'Yes,' said Hatty anxiously. 'But what had he better have to eat?'

'Oh, try something you give to sick humans,' said Mansoor. 'Something healthy and easy to eat.'

'Ice-cream?' I said, thinking back to the time I had my tonsils out.

'No, idiot. Soup or toast or something,' said Hatty.

Delicious, *said the computer screen.* **Thank you.**

'You twit,' exclaimed Hatty. 'Now he's gone and eaten the ice...' She stopped herself just in time. 'Now he's gone and eaten the whole lot!'

We looked at each other in alarm.

'Well,' said Mansoor. 'He doesn't look any the worse for it.'

Cyberpest was sitting up and looked almost cheerful.

'Oops!' I said. 'We're going to have to be very careful about what we say.'

19

Some Awkward Questions

It took several days for Cyberpest to recover. We were very strict about what he ate. Each time we fed him, we only allowed him one new food and then waited anxiously to see what effect it had on him. By the weekend we had decided he was a vegetarian. He definitely seemed worse after he ate meat.

'Poor old CP,' said Rob. 'No more burgers.'

'No more chicken nuggets either,' I agreed. 'The problem is, how are we going to tell him?'

It wasn't easy to solve. For a start, we felt awful about it. It was like having to tell a little kid that they couldn't have any Easter Eggs or something. I suddenly felt really guilty about all the hard times I'd given Mum and Dad when they wouldn't let me do something. It wasn't that they were being mean; it was just that they wanted the best for me. But that wasn't the only problem. How could we say to Cyberpest, 'No more burgers and chicken nuggets,' when the moment we said it, he'd eat it? See what I mean?

We called in Mansoor.

'Easy!' he said. 'Just try typing it into the computer.'

'I don't see why that should work,' objected Rob. 'Just 'cos that's the way he speaks to us, it doesn't mean we can speak to him like that.'

'Well, try it anyway,' said Mansoor.

So we did.

Cyberpest was busy drawing complicated multi-coloured shapes with his finger. He ignored us.

'Cyberpest,' I said sternly. He looked at me, fleetingly. We didn't normally call him Cyberpest any more. 'Don't ignore us. You're just pretending you can't read what's on the screen.

Tumpty, Tumpty, Tumpty, said the multi-coloured message on the computer screen.

'What?' said Rob.

'Crikey! Has he lost his marbles?' said Mansoor.

'Hmm...' I said. 'Two can play at that game. Come on. Let's go.'

'What?' said Rob. 'You can't just leave him on his own! Remember what happened when you left him in the bathroom. And you promised...'

'I didn't promise. Just hurry up and do as I say,' I said. 'I know what I'm doing.'

And they followed me out of the room.

You were very bossy.

Well, what else could I do? It worked, didn't it? And I didn't leave him for very long.

I know—but I'm still not sure we should have done it. Not after he asked us not to…

Look, sometimes you have to be cruel to be kind.

OK. OK. I just hope if I have any kids they're less trouble than CP.

Huh! Dream on, Rob! Can I get on with the story now?

I suppose so.

It was simple really. All this tumpty tumpty stuff was just Cyberpest pretending he couldn't hear us—you know how people sort of whistle and look the other way. He knew perfectly well what we'd written on the screen. He just didn't want to take any notice. It didn't take me long to explain to the boys—and then we went back to see how Cyberpest was getting on.

You left me on my own again, said the screen in huge letters.

'You weren't co-operating with us,' I said firmly. 'You co-operate with us and we co-operate with you—and the other way round. OK? You know what it says on the screen. You know you're not allowed to eat…'

Quick as a flash, Mansoor clapped his hand over my mouth.

'Don't say it!' he said.

'I wasn't going to,' I retorted, pulling his hand away. 'I was only going to say...'

'Well, don't,' said Mansoor. 'You're making me nervous. Just get him to read the screen.'

'He has read the screen. Haven't you, CP?'

Sulkily, Cyberpest nodded.

'So no more...'

This time Mansoor nearly throttled me.

'Will you stop nearly saying meat?' he shouted.

There was a horrified silence.

Yum, Yum, said the computer screen.

'Oh no!' Rob wailed. 'Now you'll be poorly again!'

But Cyberpest was grinning at us.

Just a joke, said the screen. **I didn't really eat it.**

'Huh,' said Rob as we all sighed with relief. 'I thought you didn't have a sense of humour.'

I'm learning, said Cyberpest.

You'll find this amazing, but with all the worry about Cyberpest, we'd forgotten that on Sunday, it was going to be Dad's birthday. We were going out for an Indian meal (much to Hatty's disgust—she doesn't like spicy food) and then on to the cinema. Mansoor was coming too. Hatty could have brought someone as well but she'd rather lost interest in everyone over the last couple of weeks.

Cyberpest liked the idea of birthdays and

spent some time trying to work out when he was due for one.

'Actually,' I admitted at last. 'I think you've missed a few. We reckon your years are about three of our days—or we did at first. You seem quite grown-up compared with us. You learned things quicker than human babies do.'

Cyberpest was very quiet and thoughtful for a long time after that. We decided to play a board-game. We were round at Mansoor's again—Mum had given up on us and had started decorating the bathroom.

Suddenly, a message appeared on the computer screen.

When do humans die? *it said.*

'It depends,' I said. 'It can happen any time. Why?'

What happens to them then?

I looked uncomfortable. 'Hatty thinks some of them go to heaven,' I said.

'So do I,' said Mansoor.

I looked at him, in surprise. 'You've never said that before,' I said.

'You never asked.'

What's heaven? *asked Cyberpest.*

We looked at each other. Hatty took a deep breath.

'No one really knows,' she said. 'But it must be all right 'cos you're with God.'

God, *said Cyberpest.* **The being that you think**

sent you here. Do you think he sent me?

'He might have,' said Hatty slowly.

Mansoor just shrugged.

'I don't know,' I said. 'I don't even know if he sent me. It's Hatty that thinks that. Maybe you're some kind of Internet baby.'

So where are you going to go when you die, Rob?

'Oh, for goodness' sake, CP. Don't get all heavy with me! I don't spend much time thinking about it, if you really want to know.'

I think you should, *said Cyberpest.*

I looked at the others for support. Now Hatty shrugged. Mansoor refused to look at me. I knew exactly whose side they were on. And it wasn't mine.

20

Lost—Again!

The next day was Sunday and Dad's birthday. At first we were too busy to notice that Cyberpest was behaving rather strangely. He'd been getting far less troublesome, partly because he was growing up and partly because we'd discovered that if you left him lying on top of a book, he sat down and read it! The only real difficulty was that when he woke in the night, he didn't want stories any more. He wanted meaningful conversation. Or at least he did with me. He probably discussed the football scores with Rob.

Not all the time. Stop trying to make me sound like a brainless jerk.

I don't have to try.

Hey! That's not fair. And if you want to know, we didn't just talk about the football scores.

So? What did you talk about?

Loads of things.

Like?

Well—cricket. Rugby. Snooker...

What about God? And where-did-we-come-from-where-are-we-going-to?

Well. A bit. It's difficult when you're half asleep.

Too right!

Oh, get on with the story, Hatty.

You started it.

No, I didn't. You made me sound like an idiot. Say sorry.

Sorry. OK?

OK.

Well, Cyberpest wouldn't settle to anything. He kept bugging me about all sorts of nonsense and demanding snacks and drinks. I put it down to being excited about Dad's birthday, but I was wrong.

Ha! Einstein admits she made a mistake!

Oh shut up, Rob! You're just cross 'cos I'm going to have to write about what a berk you were at the cinema.

No, I'm not.

Yes, you are.

No, I'm not. And who says you're going to write about it anyway?

This bit's important. I want to get it right.

Well, let me get on with it then! OK?

After a slap-up birthday meal, we went to the cinema. It was great. Cyberpest, who was lying on the arm of my seat, was riveted. Not a peep out of him for nearly two hours. I suppose that was how I came to forget about him.

I'll write that bit again. Because it's big. THAT WAS HOW I CAME TO FORGET ABOUT HIM.

It wasn't like Hatty leaving him in the bathroom. At least then we knew he was safe. This time he'd been left in a public place. And it wasn't like dropping him on the pavement. Then it had been easy enough to go back and get him. This time, we had to persuade Mum and Dad.

As we drove home, we were all chatting about the film and, of course, we try not to talk to Cyberpest when Mum and Dad are around. It suddenly occurred to me that I ought to check he was all right. After all, he hadn't said a word all evening. I reached into my pocket—and froze.

I didn't need to check my other pockets. I could see him in my mind's eye, lying on the arm of my seat. I had forgotten to pick him up.

'Hat!' I said urgently. 'I've left CP at the cinema!'

I could feel Mansoor and Hatty staring at me through the darkness in absolute horror. Then Hatty sprang into action.

'Mum! Dad! We've left Rob's old cyberpet at the cinema. Can we go back please?'

'Oh, for goodness' sake, Hatty,' said Mum, who was driving. 'No, we can't. The cinema will be shut by now. And we need to get Mansoor home. It's very late. You'll have to ring up in the morning.'

'But I can't!' wailed Hatty. 'It's school tomorrow.'

'Ring when you get home from school,' said Dad. 'It'll probably have been handed in to Lost Property. And if the worst comes to the worst, you can always save up and get a new one.'

'I can't get a new one!' Hatty was screaming now. 'That one's special. And you wouldn't let me have one when I asked before!'

'No, and we won't let you have one again, if this is how you're going to carry on! Really, Harriet. At your age. It's only a bit of plastic.'

'It's not only a bit of plastic. It's…'

I gripped her arm hard.

'Please, Dad,' I said. 'I know it's your birthday but it wouldn't take long just to nip back and have a look.'

'Yes,' said Mansoor. 'Please go back. It's not

that late really. My parents won't mind.'

'Perhaps just this once…' said Mum hesitantly.

Dad snorted. 'Give in to her, you mean?' he said. 'After that performance?'

They were acting just like Hatty and I did, trying to work out what to do when Cyberpest threw a wobbly. It would have been funny if I hadn't been so worried.

Hatty was sobbing quietly now. She knew that tantrums never worked with Mum and Dad.

'Please,' she begged quietly. 'I'm sorry I screamed at you. It wouldn't take very long.'

'Well, all right,' said Dad gruffly. 'Just this once. I don't mind, if your mother doesn't.'

Mum turned the car around.

We drew up on the double yellow lines outside the cinema.

'Hurry up!' said Mum. 'I don't want to have to go and park. Nip in and ask if they've found it. Quick! It looks like they're about to close!'

We all streamed out of the car. Mum was right. A man was just slotting the bolts home. We hammered on the doors and Dad made polite noises through the glass.

Grudgingly, the man opened the door a crack.

'We're closed,' he said forbiddingly.

'I know…' said Dad, and explained what we wanted.

'Wait here,' said the man. 'I'll ask.'

'Nora!' we heard him shout. 'Someone here wants Lost Property.'

A bustling little woman appeared through a door behind the sweet counter. Dad went through the whole story again.

'I don't think we've had one of them handed in,' she said. 'A blue glove and a spectacle case. That's all I remember from tonight. Things slip down the sides of the seats, you know. Our girls know to check. But I'll just go and see...'

I groaned. 'Down the side of one of the seats! Maybe I knocked him off the arm! Can anyone remember where we were sitting?'

'Only sort of,' said Mansoor.

Hatty hadn't a clue. Dad wasn't listening.

The woman came back. 'No, I'm sorry,' she said. 'No cyberpets at all.'

'Please,' said Hatty. 'Please could we just go and have a look? We'd be ever so quick.'

'Harriet!' said Dad warningly.

But Hatty can be very cute when she tries hard enough. The woman was softening.

'You'll have to be extremely *quick,' she said. 'These doors should have been locked five minutes ago.'*

'Oh, thank you,' breathed Hatty and we all dived through the doorway, nearly knocking over the little woman in our rush.

We had a rough idea of where we'd sat, so we

took a row each. With Dad to help, we could cover a lot of ground quite quickly. Or so we thought. A few minutes later, my hands already sore from squeezing them between seats, I was ready to give up.

'This is hopeless,' I said. 'I can't reach deep enough.'

'Well, we can check the floor as well,' said Mansoor.

'Just a minute,' said Hatty. 'Wouldn't he make a noise, if he were here?'

I shot a glance at Dad, but he was a couple of rows away and wasn't listening.

'Of course he would!' I agreed excitedly. 'You're a genius, Hatty! We're wasting our time!'

'That's all very well,' said Mansoor. 'But if he isn't here, where is he?'

21

A Scary Night

Moments later, we were back outside. The bustling manageress was sympathetic but final.

'Ring tomorrow and I'll fill in a Lost Property form,' she said. 'It's too late to get the file out now. But I think it's probably gone out with the waste, I'm afraid. Our girls are very thorough. Never mind. You can always get another one.'

There was nothing we could say to that. We climbed into the car and sat in grim silence. I just managed to remember to thank Mum and Dad for taking us back to look. The bottom had fallen out of my world. Now that Cyberpest was lost, I could have cut out my tongue for moaning at Hatty about having to look after him for the rest of my life. What were we going to do? We had to find him. If he wasn't in the cinema, he must be in the waste—and tomorrow he'd be crushed in the back of a dustcart. We couldn't just abandon him. We had to get him back. But how?

We hardly spoke as we dropped off Mansoor at his house.

'We'll think of something,' he said, as he got

out, but I couldn't imagine what. What an end to a birthday treat!

I couldn't sleep, of course. All I could think of was poor old Cyberpest all alone somewhere, wondering why we'd abandoned him again—and about to be destroyed for ever. I couldn't bear it. I turned on my stomach and sobbed into my pillow.

Which was how Hatty found me.

'Come on, Rob,' she said, shaking me. 'It's no good lying there crying. Mum and Dad are asleep now. We can go and get him.'

'What?' I snivelled. 'Don't talk rubbish, Hatty. How can we go and get him? We don't even know where he is.' I know, I know, I was being a complete wimp, but remember it was me that had left him behind.

'He must be in the rubbish,' she said, firmly. 'Where else could he be?'

'One of the cleaners might have taken him home for her kids.'

'With no battery in the back? And anyway, cyberpets are old news. No, he'll have been thrown away, I'm sure of it.'

'So how are we going to get to the cinema, Einstein?' I demanded. 'Walk?'

'Yes. It's not all that far. It shouldn't take us more than half an hour if we're quick.'

'Are you crazy? It's past midnight. We can't just go on our own! What if we got stopped by

the police? What if...' My blood ran cold at the thought of what else might happen to us.

Suddenly, Hatty was angry.

'So what are you going to do?' she hissed. 'Just lie there till morning and let CP get crushed to death when the binmen come at six o'clock? Well, go on then, if it makes you happy. But I'm going to rescue him!'

I grabbed her as she swung round. 'No, Hatty, you can't,' I said fiercely.

'Yes, Rob, I can,' she retorted, tossing back her head. 'You can't stop me. I'll just have to pray very hard.'

I got out of bed. I didn't think this was the time to start arguing with her about God. 'I'll come,' I said, wearily.

The first problem was the burglar alarm. How were we going to switch it off so we could get out of the house? Rob crept down the stairs. He had a rough idea of how to turn off the alarm. I sat on my bed and prayed.

Moments later, he was back.

'They've forgotten to switch it on!' he whispered excitedly.

'What?' I couldn't believe it. They'd done that before, especially when they'd been out late, but tonight of all nights! It was unbelievable! 'Thank you, God!' I whispered.

We decided to use the back door. There'd be

less chance of Mum and Dad hearing us. Then we set off, one at a time to stop the stairs creaking on the way down.

I can say it now. Now that it's all over. That walk through the town to the cinema was the scariest thing I've ever done. (Even what came later wasn't as bad.) At the time there wasn't a moment to think about it. But walking through those streets, trying to stay out of the glare of the street-lamps, trying to be quick but unseen, was terrifying. My heart was pounding like mad and I felt sick. But we had to keep going. At one stage, a white car zoomed towards us. I was sure it was a police car and pulled Rob into a shop doorway. I screamed. A body lay crumpled at my feet. Of course, it was a tramp, trying to find a bit of shelter. He moaned in his sleep, and I leaped away, scared stiff that I had woken him.

Rob dragged me on. Now that I had made him come, he was more determined than me. I was nearly crying with fear.

'Come on, Hat!' he urged. 'It's not far now. Especially if we use the underpass!'

'No, Rob!' I protested. 'Not the underpass!'

I hated it, even in daylight, all smelly like a public loo and covered in graffiti. But the only alternative was to cross the dual carriageway, lit up like a runway with street lights. It had to be the underpass. Don't ever think what we did was exciting. It wasn't. It was awful. My stomach churned the whole time. I had to keep telling myself that the only reason I was doing something that was so wrong and stupid, was to save Cyberpest's life. I kept praying, even though I wasn't sure God would approve. I didn't care what Rob said about it. How come he expected me to have all the answers? I mean we're talking GOD here. How was I supposed to know how he worked? I figured that if we all had to be perfect before God helped us, he'd be out of a job by now.

It wasn't far once we were through, and soon we could see the cinema. I think I felt worst of all then. Was I really going to empty the rubbish bins and search for Cyberpest? It had seemed such a good idea in the safety of my room. Now, I was shaking at the very thought. But what else could we do?

The cinema is built on a corner. Behind it, there is a small car park. I was sure I had seen bins out at the back so it wasn't as if we had to break into anywhere. In the morning, they would think it had been foxes. That's what I told myself.

'Come on then, Rob,' I said. Like me, he was hesitating.

We sneaked round to the car park. It was difficult to remain hidden—it's amazing how bright street lights can be. But we got safely to the corner of the building and peered round it.

It was hard to see for a moment. The car park

was dark and gloomy and our eyes had to adjust but, sure enough, we picked out the bins, just where I'd thought they would be.

And then I clutched Rob's arm in terror. Because right beside the bins there was a shadow. And it was moving.

'There's someone else here!' I gasped.

Rob pulled me back round the corner of the cinema.

'Ssh!' he hissed. 'He'll see you!'

'But who could it be?'

'A tramp? Someone who lives on the streets? He'll be looking for something to eat, I should think.'

'No!'

'Well, who else could it be? We'll just have to wait till he's gone.'

'I can't.' The idea of waiting on the corner for any length of time, scared me rigid.

'You'll have to.'

And then, clear as a bell, I heard it.

Bleep, bleep, bleep.

Our eyes locked.

'CP!' we both said together.

'Come on!' said Rob. 'Let's frighten that bloke away!'

He stuck his head round the corner.

'Here, you!' he shouted, in a funny, deep voice. 'What d'you think you're doing?'

The shadowy figure jumped and turned round.

'It's only a kid!' I gasped. But it wasn't any old kid...

'It's Mansoor!' exclaimed Rob, as we ran out into the car park.

'What are you...'

'Aargh,' exclaimed Mansoor. 'You nearly scared me to death. But never mind that now. Come on. Help me find CP. He's in here somewhere.'

'He's stopped bleeping,' I said.

'He's only done it a few times,' said Mansoor. 'I think he must be trying to save energy.'

'CP,' I called softly. 'Bleep again. It's me. Hatty. Rob's here too. We're trying to find you. Make some more noise.'

Bleep, bleep, bleep.

'It's coming from that big wheelie bin,' said Rob excitedly. 'Help me, Mansoor!'

Together they hauled back the huge lid and Mansoor gave Rob a leg up. Then, perched on the edge, Rob began to chuck us the black bags.

'Bleep again, CP!' I called.

'It's this one!' Rob threw down another bag.

'Careful!' I gasped, as it hit the concrete, but Mansoor was already ripping it open. We rummaged frantically through the left-over popcorn and paper cups.

Bleep, bleep, bleep.

At last! There, at the bottom of a paper tub, covered in melted ice-cream, lay Cyberpest. I snatched him up and hugged him to my chest.

'Oh, CP!' I sobbed. 'I thought we'd really lost you this time!'

'Got you!' said a stern voice, as a large hand gripped my shoulder. 'And just what d'you three think you're up to?'

22

Stop! Police!

I was too slow to run. Where we live, policemen always come in pairs, so while the first one held onto Hatty and Mansoor, the second grabbed me.

'Stop struggling, Hat!' I said. She was doing her utmost to squirm out of the policeman's grasp. 'We weren't doing anything wrong. We're not even trespassing!'

'Oh, that's something you make a habit of, is it?' said my policeman sarcastically.

'That's not what I meant.'

'No? What did you mean then? I think we'd better take you down to the station and find out.'

'But we weren't doing any harm!' protested Mansoor. He looked sick. I knew what he was thinking—exactly the same as me. Our parents were going to hit the roof.

'That remains to be seen,' said the first policeman. 'Three kids going through this rubbish at one in the morning? Looks very suspicious to me.'

'But we were only looking for our cyberpet,'

said Hatty, beginning to cry. 'We've found him now. We were just about to go home. Honestly. Look!'

She held out Cyberpest on the flat of her hand. All sticky and smeary with ice-cream, he didn't exactly look like the crown jewels. They would never believe we'd been looking for that.

My policeman took Cyberpest and flipped him over casually. 'Who are you trying to kid?' he said. 'It hasn't even got a battery in it.'

'Hasn't it?' I said, trying to sound surprised. 'It must have fallen out.'

The policeman looked at me very hard indeed. 'Right,' he said. 'Of course. So it must. I think we've spent long enough here. You put these three in the car, Kev, and I'll have a good look round. Oh, and take this!'

He flipped Cyberpest up into the air. Quick as a flash, Hatty put out her hand and grabbed him. The policeman called Kev was too slow. Cyberpest was back with Hatty.

'Hand it over, there's a good girl,' said Kev patiently.

'No,' said Hatty. 'He's mine.'

The policeman sighed. 'Have it your own way, then,' he said, sounding bored. 'But we'll need to have a good look at it down at the station. Take it apart. See what's inside.'

That was the moment that Hatty went crazy. Kev wasn't holding onto her any more. Let's face it, she's only small and she looked petrified. But, of course, she wasn't petrified of him—only of what might happen to Cyberpest.

She ran. Now, if you remember, she can move pretty fast—and she was saving Cyberpest's life. Or that's how she saw it. She was out on the main road before Kev had worked out what was happening.

Mansoor and I were more with it. I went one way. Mansoor went another. Three kids. Two policemen. Surely Hatty could get away?

'The girl!' yelled Kev's mate, as he bounded after Mansoor. 'Follow the girl!'

But Kev was after me and gaining fast.

'Got you!' he gasped and I lurched forward as he grabbed my jacket.

Mansoor is a good runner but it was only moments before he'd been caught too. Hatty, however, had disappeared.

'Get them in the car!' said my policeman. 'The girl can't have got far. And even if she's telling the truth, she shouldn't be running about on her own at this time of night.'

Too right. I was scared stiff. So I did what Hatty would have done; I prayed. 'Please God, keep Hatty safe,' I muttered, over and over again.

The police car shot forward. My policeman was speaking into the radio, putting out an alert for Hatty. It was terrible. I was desperate for her to be safe—but I didn't want the police finding her—not with Cyberpest.

'Can't you just take us home?' It was Mansoor. 'We don't normally do this sort of thing. We really were looking for that cyberpet. Honestly.'

'I believe you,' said my policeman. 'But the question is, why? And who for? What's so special about that cyberpet? Looks innocent enough, doesn't it? But I wonder what might be hidden inside it?' He looked at us meaningfully.

So that was what this was all about! They thought we'd been sent by someone to pick something up—drugs or stolen goods, I suppose. My heart sank. What had we got ourselves into? It felt unreal—like it was a television programme and we'd been sucked in.

When we arrived at the police station, we were led through a maze of corridors and handed over to a tall, grey-haired policewoman. She seemed to be more important than the men who had brought us in, but she was kind and friendly and even found us some biscuits. We were introduced to a young man who told us he was a social worker and that he would be with us until our parents arrived. I began to feel much better—until the policewoman asked us for the names and addresses of our parents.

I hesitated.

'Come on,' she said. 'The sooner we talk to them, the sooner we can get all this sorted out.'

Reluctantly, we told her, and Kev, who was still with us, hurried off with the information. I imagined the phone ringing at home and Mum or Dad staggering down to answer it. I imagined their horror at hearing where I was and worse—that Hatty was on her own somewhere in the town centre. My lips began to tremble and I dug my fists into my eyes.

And then—thank God! Away in the distance, muffled by doors and corridors, I could hear Hatty. She was in full cry and coming nearer.

'No! No! He's mine! Give him back! I won't let you take him apart. Give him back! Give him back!'

'Excuse me a moment,' said the policewoman and she stepped out of the room. Moments later, she was back, leading a tear-stained, sobbing Hatty by the hand. She laid Cyberpest on the table. Hatty pulled away from her and ran to me.

'They're going to kill CP!' she sobbed.

'It'll be OK,' I said helplessly.

'No, it won't,' stormed Hatty. 'Not if they take him apart!'

The policewoman looked puzzled. 'We only need a quick look,' she said gently. 'And we can put it together again easily, I'm sure. And it doesn't seem to be working anyway.'

'But you don't understand...' wailed Hatty.

'Look,' said the policewoman. 'I'm sure there's no real problem here. We just need to

do a quick check to be on the safe side. Then your parents will be here; we can check out a few details, and you can all go home to bed. Wouldn't that be nice?'

'But…'

But the policewoman had made up her mind. She passed Cyberpest to Kev. 'Get this checked over quickly,' she said. 'And I mean quickly. And make sure it comes back in one piece.' Then she turned back to us. 'Now,' she said, briskly. 'Let's just fill in a few forms, shall we?'

Behind the policewoman and the social worker, there was a computer. It had a rather jolly screen-saver—a burglar with a bag of swag being endlessly chased by a gang of policemen. I watched it, mesmerized. And then suddenly, I nearly leaped out of my chair. For the briefest of moments, the screen went black and Cyberpest was there smiling at me. I shook myself—I must have been drowsing off—imagining I could see him. But when I glanced sideways at the others, they looked as dumbstruck as me. We all stared rigidly at the screen. Seconds later, it happened again.

'It's…' said Hatty and stopped herself.

'What?' said the policewoman, looking up.

'Nothing,' said Hatty. 'I just coughed.'

The screen went black again.

It's OK, *said the multi-coloured message.* **I'm in here.**

And suddenly, once again, for a split second, Cyberpest himself appeared on the screen.

My brain was working overtime. So Cyberpest had moved! The case wasn't the real him at all. The real him was something else—something that didn't need a case. So now he was in the computer! Wow! I wanted to jump up and down, it was so exciting!

Hatty was sitting staring at the screen with her mouth hanging open. Her face looked as if a million lightbulbs had been switched on inside. Mansoor was shaking his head from side to side in stunned amazement.

And then the bubble burst. The door opened and in walked Kev. He handed the empty cyber-pet case to the policewoman.

'Nothing,' he said. But there was no time to feel relieved because, right behind him, were the people we least wanted to see in the whole world. Our parents.

23

Over to You

Mum took one look at Hatty and threw her arms round her.

'Thank God!' she kept saying, over and over again, tears pouring down her cheeks. 'Thank God you're safe!'

Dad came over and hugged me against his chest. He looked old, anxious and grey.

'What's all this about then, Rob?' he said gruffly, and I could tell he too was trying hard not to cry. It was terrible. I'd have felt far better if they'd been angry. But, of course, they were even more delighted to see us safe and sound than we had been to find Cyberpest safe and sticky at the bottom of that ice-cream tub.

'We were just trying to find CP—Hatty's cyberpet, I mean,' I said lamely. 'She was sure he was in the rubbish—and we didn't want the binmen to get him.'

Dad shook his head in bewilderment. 'But I thought that craze was over!' he said. 'I always knew they were a bad idea. I should never have let you buy one. How can you get so attached to a bit of plastic?'

There was no way of explaining. I shrugged helplessly. Mum, who had stopped slobbering all over Hatty, chipped in.

'But it was very brave,' she said gently. 'And kind. Boys aren't usually so nice to their little sisters.'

'It was downright stupid,' said Dad. 'Anything could have happened.'

'I'm sorry, Dad,' I said. 'I never meant all this to happen. I never meant to end up in the police station.'

'Don't blame Rob,' said Hatty. 'It was my idea. I made him do it. I'm sorry.'

'Humph,' grunted Dad. 'I might have known.'

And then Mansoor's dad arrived. His mum had stayed at home with his sisters. Kev was sent to get tea and more biscuits. Suddenly everything felt much better. All our parents looked so anxious and respectable—especially Dad with his stripy pyjamas poking out from under his sweater—that the idea of us being caught up in some shady drugs deal seemed ridiculous. Somehow, Kev had managed to unearth some chocolate digestives and they helped a lot. Everyone began to talk and apologize and laugh, even though the police were still asking questions and filling in forms.

'Well,' said the policewoman, before things got too merry. 'I think we have all the details we need. You can go home now and we'll contact

you when we've completed our investigations.'

I felt a sudden cold chill in my stomach. So it hadn't finished yet. I suppose the policewoman wanted to scare us a bit. I mean, we had done something very stupid. And we'd wasted a lot of police time. Could they lock you up for that?

'But we haven't done anything really bad,' protested Hatty. (There's no putting that kid down.)

Kid? Who are you calling a kid?

Oh, don't start, Hatty. Not now! We're nearly at the end of the story!

Well, let me have a go then. You've been rabbiting on for ages.

Oh, all right. Go on then.

OK, so then the policewoman gave me a really steely look.

'I hope to make sure, young lady,' she said, 'that you never do anything worse. There won't be any chocolate biscuits if I see you in here again.'

And she glared at all three of us, in a way which made me glad I wasn't a real criminal.

But there was one last thing to be sorted out.

'If we're going home now,' I said loudly, 'I need my cyberpet back. Please.'

'Oh, that. Well, we certainly don't need that

any more.' And she handed the case over to me.

I could feel Rob and Mansoor staring. We all wanted to know the same thing. Where was Cyberpest? Had he come back? Or was he still in the police computer?

I looked down at the black screen.

'CP,' I breathed. 'Are you there?'

And, for a split second, there he was in glowing multi-colours, back in my hand.

I let out a huge sigh of relief. 'It's OK,' I said. 'He's back.'

And if the grown-ups thought I was crazy, I didn't care tuppence.

And that was almost that. The next day was Monday and we should have been back at school, but Mum and Dad stayed at home and we all slept late. Then, of course, we had to face the music. I won't go into all the details. I'm sure you know just how bad you can feel when you've *really* upset your parents. There was one awful moment when I thought Dad was going to take Cyberpest off me—but Mum stopped him.

'No,' she said. 'I think it would be a good thing to let her keep it. Let's see if she can play with it *responsibly* from now on. Without letting it take over her life quite so much. Hatty's getting quite grown-up for her age. I think we need to take more account of that.'

I nearly cheered! At last! They finally seemed

to have noticed! But I nearly cried as well. I mean, how much more responsibly can you play with a cyberpet that's real? How can you stop it taking over your life? I couldn't see how I was going to manage that. It was Cyberpest himself who sorted it out.

I know you've only had a short go but can I write a bit now? It's not fair if you write all the rest.

I wasn't going to. And, anyway, it's making me want to cry already.

Right then, it was like this.

As soon as Mum and Dad had finished with us, Cyberpest, who had been very quiet, began to bleep. He was sitting in the middle of his screen looking very agitated and pointing to his mouth.

'Are you hungry, CP?' I asked, puzzled.

He shook his head.

'Stupid!' said Hatty. 'He wants to talk to us. Don't you, CP?'

Cyberpest nodded.

'Can it wait?' I asked.

Cyberpest shook his head.

I sighed. There was nothing else for it. I crept into the kitchen where Mum and Dad were drinking coffee.

'Mum. Dad. Please may we have a little go

on the computer?'

They looked at one another.

'Well, I don't mind,' said Dad. 'What do you think?'

Mum nodded. 'Not for long, mind you. I suppose it's got to be better than playing with that cyberpet.'

Little did she know. I nearly laughed, except that I still felt pretty glum from the telling-off we'd had. I raced upstairs to tell Hatty.

Moments later we were hunched over the computer.

I'll do this bit. OK?

Oh, all right then. Go on.

Suddenly, to our amazement, instead of just a technicolor message, Cyberpest appeared on the computer screen. Then he disappeared and *then* we got our message.

I can change bodies, *he said.* **Look!**

And suddenly, there he was, back in the cyberpet. And then back on the computer screen.

'Wow!' said Rob. 'And that's what you did at the police station. When did you find out you could do that?'

When they were going to take me apart. I had to think of something. And I just thought it might work.

'But how?' I breathed.

I don't know. I just hoped I would move to the computer and it worked. Good job it did.

'Did it feel funny?' I asked. 'Weren't you scared?'

Both, said Cyberpest. **I thought I wasn't going to make it for a moment. But I'm OK, you see. The real me isn't anything to do with the body I'm in.**

'Crikey!' said Rob. 'You were brave.'

No choice, said Cyberpest.

'But it was like us *dying*!' I gasped. 'I mean, you had no idea if you were going to end up where you wanted to be, or not!'

Sort of, agreed Cyberpest. **Except that I'm still here on earth. You won't be.**

'What?'

When you die. You won't still be here.

'Well, our bodies will...' said Rob rather uncomfortably.

'Oh shut up, Rob,' I interrupted impatiently. 'He doesn't mean our bodies, do you CP? You mean...'

I mean the real you will be somewhere else. So maybe you'd better try to find out where you're going. And so had I.

'Well, I suppose so,' said Rob hesitantly. 'But how?'

Well I don't know what you're going to do. But I'm moving on.

'What?' We spoke together.

I'm going to go. Look at the trouble I've caused.

I need to keep searching. Find out where I've come from. Where I'm going to.

'But how?' (It's me, Rob, writing now. Hatty's beginning to snivel.)

Take me down to a toy shop and I'll move. Easy. OK?

'NO!' Hatty grabbed the keyboard in both hands and screamed at the screen.

I didn't say anything. It took me a moment or two to understand what CP meant.

'I don't want you to go!' cried Hatty in a terrible voice. 'I said I'd be your Mummy. I love you CP!'

The writing on the screen wobbled a bit.

I love you too, Hatty. But kids move on. I've got to go.

'But we've only just got you back!'

I know. And I never said thank you. I'm sorry.

Hatty gulped hard. 'When will you go?' she croaked.

Now. Before I change my mind.

'But what about Mansoor? You can't go without saying goodbye! And Mum and Dad won't let us go off to a toy shop just like that!' She was playing for time.

I could barely speak but I said it anyway. 'We can ring Mansoor. Tell him to meet us at the newsagent's near his house. That's where I bought Cyberpest in the first place. They've still got some. And game-boys and things. You could try something different this time.'

'But you might get killed!' Hatty was really crying now.

I nearly got killed with you. But I didn't.

'But we understood you, we were nice to you, we...'

'Threw him under a car?'

Hatty turned on me. She looked like she was ready to kill me.

'I hate you!' she stormed. 'Don't you want him to stay? Don't you love him?'

I grabbed her by the arms. 'Of course I do, stupid!' I said, trying to stay calm. 'But that doesn't mean it's right to keep him. We've got to let him go, Hat. He's right. He needs to move on. So do we. Be honest. He can't do much worse with someone else.'

Hatty's whole body seemed to sag. She pulled herself away from me and turned back to the screen.

'Say you'll come back to us one day!' she begged.

No. Then you'd spend your whole life waiting for me. You've got more important things to think about.

'Oh CP, you sound so grown-up! Just two weeks ago, you were a baby!'

'I'll go and ring Mansoor,' I said. I couldn't bear it. I just wanted to get it over with.

Ten minutes later, Rob was dragging me out of

the house. I was bawling for all I was worth.

'Come on, Hat,' he said, putting his arm round me. 'Mum and Dad will wonder what on earth I'm doing to you.'

I made a bit of an effort. 'Let's run then,' I said.

Mansoor was waiting for us. He looked tired and anxious. Without a word, I handed Cyberpest over to him. He turned away.

'Bye, CP,' we heard him say. 'It's been great knowing you. I'm glad you got better.'

He whispered something we couldn't hear. Then he handed him back.

I passed him to Rob.

He took a deep breath. 'Goodbye CP. All the best with your search. I'll be searching too from now on. Honest. You've made me think about things I've never bothered with before.'

And then it was my turn. I gazed down at the little figure on the screen. His head was covered in wobbly little spikes. A tear splashed down onto his floor.

'You can change your mind, CP,' I said hopefully.

He shook his head.

I put the screen to my mouth and kissed it. 'I love you CP. But I know why you're going. And I won't forget all the things you've said. You never know—maybe one day we'll meet again.' I was too choked to say any more. 'God bless,'

I whispered.

He waved a hand. And then the screen went black.

We walked into the shop.

Slowly, we made our way to the computer toys. I laid Cyberpest down gently next to them. We watched. And waited. And suddenly, instead of being black, Cyberpest's screen was the normal grey colour. Hesitantly, I picked it up.

'CP?' I whispered. 'Are you there?'

Nothing. He had gone.

'Put it back,' said Rob gently. 'It isn't him any more. And we don't want the shopkeeper thinking we've nicked something.'

'But…' But I knew he was right. The real CP had gone. And I hadn't even found out where he'd come from. Or why.

'Goodbye, CP,' I said out loud. 'Wherever you are. Take care.'

Wherever you are.

Wherever he is.

Wherever he's going.

Maybe, one day, he'll visit you. Look after him for us. Please.